T0356035

Elly's
Plate

Plant-based Comfort
Food Made Easy

Elly's Plate

ELLY SMART

[RED]

PHOTOGRAPHY BY JO SIDEY

Introduction
6

How to Use this Book
8

Getting to Grips with the Basics
12

Other Useful
Ingredients
13

Meat
Alternatives
14

Dairy
Alternatives
16

Useful
Equipment
17

Morning Plates

18

Small Plates

40

Quick Plates

66

Prepped Plates

90

Protein-Packed Plates

122

Comforting Plates

144

Messy Plates

176

Sweet Plates

198

Index
217

Thank You
221

About the Author
222

Introduction

Usually, cookbook authors introduce themselves by saying that they grew up always cooking and that a natural cheffy flair runs through their veins. As a kid, my favourite dinner was a Chicago Town frozen pizza and I'd be pretty happy with just a ham sandwich when staying at my Grannie Mary's house. When I went to university and had to start cooking for myself, I had four meals in my repertoire that never failed me: spag bol, carbonara, an omelette and, the old faithful, sausage and mash. Back then, I was a pretty big meat eater and not particularly creative in the kitchen.

As the years passed and I learned more about where my food came from (and watched one too many enlightening documentaries) I reached a turning point and decided that I couldn't in good conscience keep putting meat on my plate. I went vegetarian and quite quickly afterwards decided to become vegan. In 2016, being vegan wasn't commonplace yet and, to begin with, I found it really tricky – mainly because I lacked so much creativity when it came to cooking. I lived with five other girls at the time, who were all fairly skeptical of my diet switch. It became my mission to step out of my comfort zone so I could convince them otherwise. I started cooking for the whole house knowing that if I could win the girls over with a vegan dish then it meant it was a 10/10 recipe. As I experimented more and more, my confidence in the kitchen grew and I discovered a whole new side to myself and my cooking abilities. The hardest part of these early days was visiting my boyfriend's house of seven boys – I'd hide the packet of Linda McCartney sausages I brought with me so they wouldn't make fun of me. I felt so proud the day I opened their freezer to discover it was packed with them because "they're only £1 and actually taste alright..."

When I graduated with my law degree and got a (very stressful) job as a paralegal, the kitchen quickly became my sanctuary. Underpaid and overworked; the only thing that took my mind off it all was cooking. When I eventually realized I needed to quit law, I got the first hospitality job I could find to pay the rent, which just so happened to be in a vegan donut shop. The owners really championed my love for cooking and eventually I gained enough confidence to start my Instagram page.

You'll have to excuse the cliché, but I finally felt like I had found myself. I had fallen fully in love with food and cooking and realized it was the only thing I wanted to do. I applied for countless roles to become a development chef and eventually somewhere took a chance on me. My time at The Vurger Co taught me so much: from designing menus, to sourcing ingredients and training staff. I got the chance to develop their sauces, which were later sold in supermarkets; design and serve their menu to hundreds of people at food festivals; and, most importantly, develop a lot of vegan burger recipes! Throughout this time, I was posting online as a hobby and outlet, never taking it too seriously.

In 2023, I decided to take a leap of faith and try making food content creation my full-time job. My following was small, but my ambitions and passion were huge! I shared recipes for meat alternatives, vegan Christmas dishes and, of course, vegan burgers, and it resonated with so many of you. My most cherished comment so far is "your food feels like walking into my favourite family restaurant" and that's exactly what I want each page of the book to feel like. So here are 80 of my best ever recipes, from my plate to yours.

How to Use this Book

I wanted every chapter in this book to have its own purpose, and I didn't want to pad out the pages with a drinks and sauces section that you'd never reach for! I've outlined each chapter below so you know which section to turn to depending on your current needs and cravings.

The Useful Bits

At the top of each recipe page you'll find a handy guide providing the prep and cook time, difficulty level and protein count.

- *The difficulty rating ranges from 1–5. A recipe that has a rating of 1/5 is so easy you could do it with your eyes closed. A recipe that has a rating of 5/5 will take a little more focus, but is still easy to achieve in a normal kitchen with minimal equipment.*
- *Protein information is given to the nearest decimal place in grams and the nearest 1/16 in ounces (below 1oz). Use grams for the most precise measurement.*
- *Any other notes that I think are useful I've popped at the bottom of each page.*
- *Every single recipe has a photo, so you can feel confident recreating them.*

1 – Morning Plates

Within this chapter you'll find 8 recipes, with 5 variations to suit every palate. All the breakfast bases are covered here: quick or slow mornings, sweet and savoury dishes, protein-packed options (try my chocolate pudding protein pots on page 39) and even meal-preppable recipes for when you're in a hurry (try my sausage mockmuffin on page 34).

2 – Small Plates

I've given you 10 recipes to whip out whenever you need to elevate your dinner party, jazz up your midweek meals, or impress your friends at aperitivo hour. Want to pack even more flavour into your favourite noodle recipes? Top those noods with my nutty smashed cucumbers (page 51). Need to add some quick greens to your fave mac and cheese? Throw in my cheesy kale (page 54). Want to whip up delicious nibbly bits for friends? Look no further than my lemon pepper mushroom wings (page 46) or crispy spiced filo rolls (page 48).

3 – Quick Plates

This will be the chapter you reach for time and time again when you need quick nourishment – 9 recipes, all taking less than 10 mins to prep and a maximum of 30 minutes to cook. All the recipes in this chapter are ordered by the time they take to make. So, if you've only got 10 minutes, start at the beginning of the chapter with my kimchi beans (page 70); if you've got 20 minutes head to the middle of the chapter and make my 'nduja flatbreads (page 77); or when you've got 30 minutes to spare go for gochujang and black bean loaded sweet potatoes (page 89).

4 – Prepped Plates

This is probably my fave chapter in the whole book – and it will be yours too if you're bored of your regular meal prep. One of my three "core" recipes is all you'll need to prep on a Sunday night to have a variety of easy and delicious suppers the following week. Make my tofu chorizo (page 95) and you're set for chorizo style tacos (page 96), chorizo chilli (page 100) and a delicious smoky chorizo burger (page 102).

5 – Protein-Packed Plates

This one is pretty self explanatory – at least 20% of the calories from every recipe in this chapter is made up of protein. Perfect for post-gym meals, all of these recipes are super satiating and fresh. If you want to prep meals for the week, make my peanut + sesame soba salad (page 136) or reset quinoa bowl (page 126); for a hearty and comforting plate try my green skillet lasagne (page 142).

6 – Comforting Plates

I wanted this chapter to feel like a big hug from your besties, and all of these recipes are best enjoyed with the people you love. Make my giant Wellington (page 162) as the centrepiece for a Sunday roast or whip up my cheesy ramen (page 148) for low-effort cosy nights in.

7 – Messy Plates

I started my food career by developing vegan burgers, so it only felt right that they had their own chapter! Filled with 8 of my ride or die recipes, these burgers and sandwiches will see you through the week and all the way into the weekend. There's a big misconception that burgers are wildly decadent and only to be enjoyed as a treat, but my barbie beet burger (page 186) or smoky pulled aubergine burger (page 197) pack a veggie punch. However, when you really do want to indulge, there's nothing better than the saucy stack in my buffalo shroom burger (page 189) or the ultimate smash burger (page 194).

8 – Sweet Plates

Sweet tooth or not, these recipes will satisfy your sugar-cravings while nourishing your soul, offering more than just a sugary hit. Need a quick treat? Whip up a batch of my lemon drizzle chia cookies (page 204). Got friends round for a movie night? Make my miso + pecan skillet cookie (page 211) for everyone to dig in to. Or, if you really wanna pull out all the stops, my end of night espresso martini chocolate churros are a MUST (page 214).

Getting to Grips *with* the Basics

Discovering how to nail the balance between salt, fat, acid, and heat was integral in levelling up my plant-based cooking (shoutout to Samin Nosrat). The staples below build the foundation for all of my recipes.

Salt
Ditch the table salt unless you're cooking pasta. You'll be amazed what a good-quality flaky salt can do – the additional texture alone can elevate a dish.

Fat
Use **good-quality olive oil** for cooking and extra virgin olive oil for drizzling. Olive oil is full of anti-inflammatory properties and makes pretty much everything taste better. **Vegan butter** is really easy to find in most supermarkets. Try to buy the variety in blocks (page 16).

Acid
For me, the zest of **lemons** and **limes** is just as important as the juice, so ensure you buy unwaxed (also, the wax sometimes contains shellac or beeswax, so is not strictly vegan). I use a range of **vinegars** in this book. Make sure you have balsamic vinegar, white and red wine vinegar and rice wine vinegar in your cupboard to get you started.

Heat
This obviously refers to the method in which a dish is cooked, but can also refer to the chilli-heat within a dish. I always have **chilli oil, chilli jam, sweet chilli sauce** and **sriracha** in my cupboard and use them a lot in my recipes, so be sure to stock up (just check the label to ensure they are vegan).

Elly's Plate

Plant-based Comfort Food Made Easy

Other Useful Ingredients

Herbs and Spices
Dried herbs and spices are the key flavour building blocks in most of my recipes. My most-used are: smoked paprika, dried oregano, ground cumin and ground coriander.

Miso Paste
An umami-packed soy paste that vegans love (and for good reason!). It's fermented and salty so it will add a mixture of tang and deep savouriness to your dishes. You can find it in the world foods section of most supermarkets.

Marmite
This is a yeast extract (not to be confused with nutritional yeast) in the form of a super-savoury and salty spread. It can add amazing depth when looking to replicate beef-like flavours.

Vegan Beef or Chicken Stock Cubes
These "meaty" stock alternatives are readily available in the UK, but if you don't have them in your country, don't worry, vegetable stock cubes or stock pots work fine too.

Agave Syrup + Maple Syrup
Both are fantastic replacements for honey to add sweetness to recipes. Maple is a little more pourable and subtle in flavour, whereas agave is thicker and stickier.

Beans + Pulses
You name it, I use it! Chickpeas, butter beans, black beans, lentils... I recommend buying the highest quality you can afford, as it makes such a difference to the bean texture and the quality of the stock. Look for beans in jars instead of cans – I really love Bold Bean Co.

Nutritional Yeast
The most fundamental staple in any vegan pantry. A deactivated yeast packed with B12 that provides a savoury, Parmesan-style flavour.

Nori
A dried edible seaweed used in some of my recipes to replicate a "fishy" taste. It's nutrient dense and also a tasty snack!

Black Salt (Kala Namak)
Due to its high sulphur content, this salt has a really "eggy" flavour. It's an acquired taste, so it's an optional extra in my egg-replacement recipes.

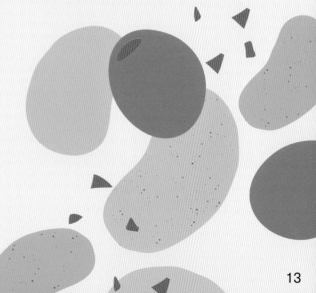

Meat
Alternatives

Mushrooms
My favourite non-processed meat alternative. For more of a "bite" I use **oyster** mushrooms. For a crispy crunch I use **shiitake** mushrooms. You can find these mushrooms in most supermarkets now, but I tend to source them from my local greengrocer or Asian supermarket.

Tofu
I use a lot of tofu in this book! It's my protein of choice because it's cheap, widely accessible, and super-versatile. If I refer to **extra-firm**, it's the type that's been vac-packed, usually in minimal water, and is harder to tear apart. If I refer to **medium-firm**, this is the type in water, that still holds its shape but has a bit more of a jiggle to it. You'll need to drain both of these before using – I also like to pat the tofu dry with paper towels. If I refer to **silken tofu**, this is the much softer, blendable type with lots of jiggle – it's also often shelf-stable so a handy one to keep in your cupboards. You'll also notice I use **smoked tofu** sometimes to add extra depth of flavour.

Tempeh
Tofu's chunkier cousin, tempeh is another age-old plant-based protein source and tends to be more of an acquired taste, so it only pops up a few times in this book (and it can be subbed for tofu if you'd prefer).

Textured Vegetable Protein (TVP)
This dehydrated soy protein is a necessity in my cupboards. It acts as a minced (ground) beef alternative and is shelf-stable so keeps for ages. It absorbs any flavour you soak it in and is super-protein dense (with over 50g/2oz of protein per 100g/3½oz of TVP). You can buy it in all different sizes, but in this book I only use the fine mince (ground meat) variant.

Vegan Mince
In addition to TVP, I also use "ready to use" vegan mince (ground vegan meat) in a few recipes. The alternatives we now have at our disposal are super-impressive at mimicking the real deal.

Vegan Sausages
When a recipe calls for vegan sausages, choose those that are "meaty" and pliable, and that come in casings you can easily remove. These give the most versatility and will help you get the best out of the recipes that use them. When using a mock meat, I will often pair it with a goodness boost from a whole food ingredient such as lentils or beans.

Vegan Chicken
I have a seitan chicken recipe on page 113 that you can use for a number of recipes in this book, but if you're short on time you can use store-bought vegan chicken pieces instead. I like to use soy- or pea-based options with minimal ingredients – these can usually be found in both the chilled and frozen aisles of supermarkets.

Vital Wheat Gluten
I only use this twice in the book: for my seitan chicken (page 113) and for my ultimate smash burger (page 194). It's high in protein and gluten, enabling it to form meat-like strands when kneaded.

Dairy Alternatives

For almost every dairy product (milk, cream, yogurt, butter) there are now a multitude of incredible vegan alternatives, many of which you would struggle to tell didn't actually contain dairy.

Milk + Cream
I switch between unsweetened soy and oat milk. When it comes to cream I switch it up – Elmlea double (heavy) vegan cream and Oatly crème fraîche are both great options.

Butter
My favourite vegan butter to use is the salted block variety (I use Naturli'), as it has a better flavour.

Yogurt
You can never go wrong with a thick Greek-style vegan yogurt! Try a few to find out your faves.

Cheese
Let's talk about it! Vegan cheese has a bit of an acquired taste, which is why I always pair it with other flavour boosters in my recipes so it's not overpowering. Try a couple of different ones until you find one you like. In this book I mostly use a meltable vegan Cheddar or a vegan feta. As a rough guide, coconut oil-based options melt really well, whereas nut-based options usually have a slightly richer taste. If you'd rather make your own, try my cashew Parm (page 61), tofu feta (page 126) or whipped ricotta (page 22).

Useful Equipment

Scales, Measuring Cups + Spoons

Buying yourself some decent measuring equipment will help you get the most out of this book. I've used teaspoon and tablespoon measurements where possible for my quicker recipes and scales for the ones that take a little more time. All measurements are given in metric first, then in imperial or cups in brackets afterwards – use just one set of measurements.

Mixing Bowls

Trust me, grab a couple of the cheapest metal mixing bowls in a few different sizes and they'll last you forever. They are really handy for almost every recipe in this book.

Wooden Chopping Board

A daily essential that I would be lost without. You don't have to splash out on one, but I find having a large wooden board makes kitchen prep much easier.

Good Quality Knives

One small serrated paring knife and a 20cm (8in) chef's knife is pretty much all you need in life, so it's worth spending a little extra on them! A smaller 10cm (4in) knife is also nice to have, but not essential.

Microplane

One of my favourite inexpensive kitchen items – perfect for speedily mincing garlic and ginger as well as adding a shower of plant-based cheese to pasta dishes.

Julienne Peeler

Not a necessity, but using it to slice your veg into ribbons makes your plate look extra-pretty. It's a cheap and cheerful addition to your kitchen gadgets drawer, and perfect for making slaw.

Non-stick Pans

For my day-to-day cooking I always reach for a non-toxic, non-stick saucepan and frying pan. They work for everything! An ovenproof option is even better – you'll need one for some of my one-pan recipes, which go straight from stovetop to oven.

Air Fryer

My air fryer definitely gets a lot of use in my kitchen! If a recipe can be made in an air fryer, as well as in the oven or a frying pan, I've provided instructions on how to do this.

High Speed Blender

This is the kitchen appliance I use nearly every day. Invest in a good one and it'll last forever and make your kitchen life so much easier. I've got one of those short stumpy blender cups that is perfect for blending thick mixes. If yours is much bigger, you may need to give some of these recipes a bit of extra blitzing to get them smooth, scraping down the sides occasionally.

Mini Chopper or Food Processor

I developed this entire book with a cheap mini chopper, so a food processor is definitely nice to have but not a necessity!

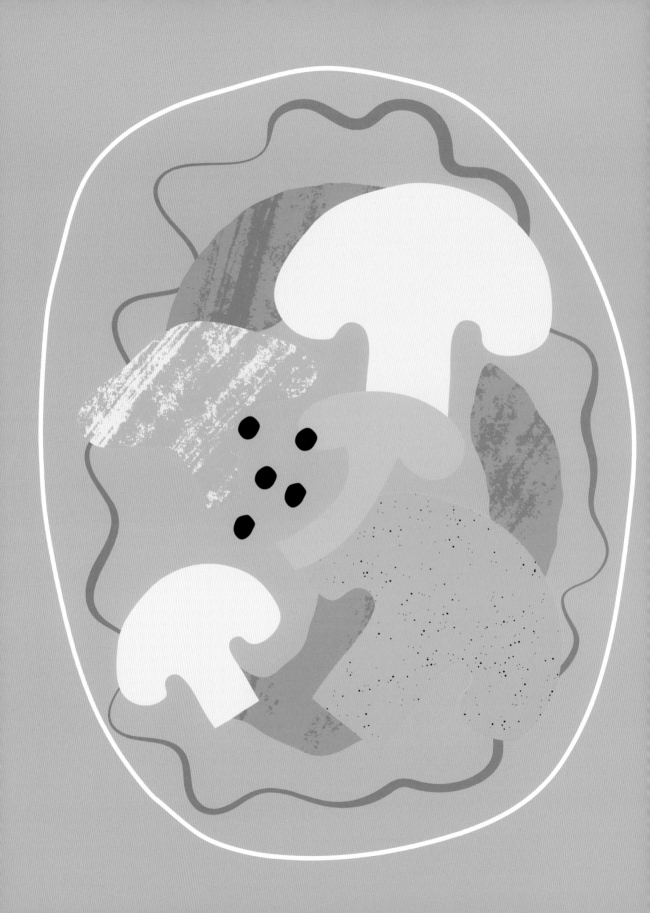

1

Morning Plates

For rushed weekday mornings or slow leisurely weekends, these recipes have got you covered.

Whipped Ricotta Toast

Caprese Style
Balsamic Strawberry
Citrus Sumac

22

Peaches + Cream Pancakes

24

One Pan Full English

26

Boozy Butter Beans + Greens

30

Breakfast Frittata

32

Smoky Sausage Mockmuffins

34

Rice Paper Omelette

Cheesy Pesto
Loaded + Spicy

37

Chocolate Protein Pots

39

Ricotta prep	Toppers	Difficulty level	Protein per slice
12 mins	5–30 mins	1/5	1: 12.7g ($\frac{7}{16}$oz)
			2: 12.8g ($\frac{7}{16}$oz)
			3: 12.9g ($\frac{7}{16}$oz)

Whipped Ricotta Toast (+ 3 toppers)

Makes about 300g (10½oz) *(enough for 6 slices of toast)*

Place the almonds in a heatproof bowl and cover them with hot water from the kettle. Leave them to soften for 10 minutes then drain. Add the softened almonds to a food processor or blender along with all the other ingredients. Blitz until smooth then taste for seasoning, adding extra salt and pepper if needed. In a sealed container this will keep in the fridge for 5 days.

WHIPPED RICOTTA

60g (2oz) flaked (slivered) almonds
150g (5½oz) medium-firm tofu, drained
3½ tbsp soy yogurt
juice of ½ lemon
1 garlic clove
3 tbsp nutritional yeast
1 tsp apple cider vinegar
½ tsp white miso paste
½ tsp salt
¼ tsp white pepper

Balsamic Strawberry Topper [1]

Makes 2 slices

120g strawberries, washed, hulled and halved or quartered
1 tsp balsamic vinegar
1½ tsp agave syrup
100g (3½oz) whipped ricotta (see above)
2 slices of sourdough bread, toasted
small handful of mint leaves

Add the strawberries to a bowl with the vinegar and agave and mix thoroughly. Leave to macerate for at least 30 minutes. Spread the toasted sourdough with the whipped ricotta then pile on the strawberries and top with some mint leaves.

Caprese-Style Topper [2]

Makes 2 slices

2 slices of sourdough bread, toasted
100g (3½oz) whipped ricotta (see above)
1 beef tomato, thinly sliced
pinch of flaky sea salt
drizzle of balsamic glaze
small handful of basil leaves

Spread the toasted sourdough with the whipped ricotta then layer on the tomato slices. Generously salt the tomatoes then drizzle with balsamic glaze and scatter with basil leaves.

Citrus Sumac Topper [3]

Makes 2 slices

2 slices of sourdough bread, toasted
100g (3½oz) whipped ricotta (see above)
1 orange, peeled and thinly sliced
½ tsp sumac
small handful of thyme leaves
drizzle of agave syrup

Spread the toasted sourdough with the whipped ricotta then layer on the orange slices. Sprinkle with sumac and thyme leaves then drizzle over a little agave syrup.

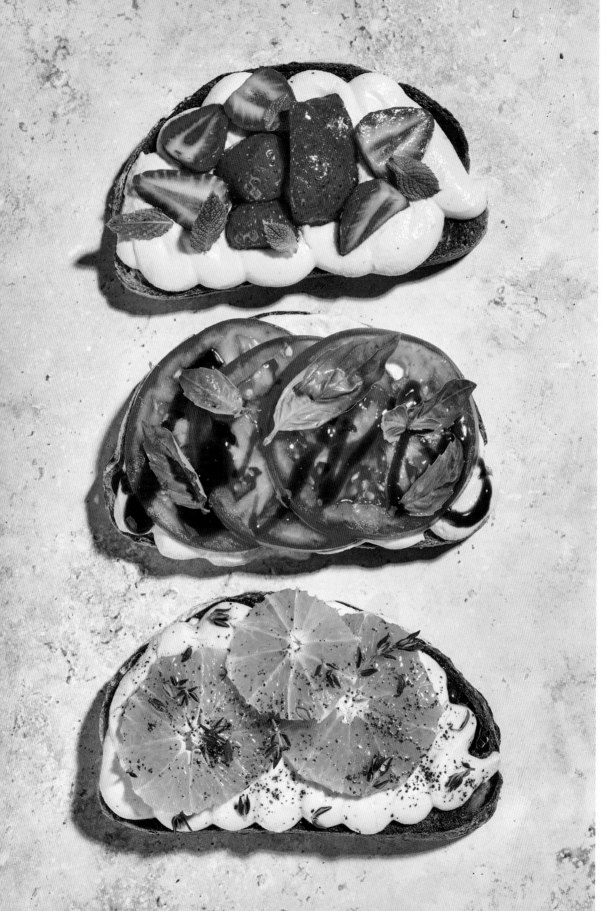

Prep	Cook	Difficulty level	Protein per serving
10 mins	15 mins	3/5	14.3g (½oz)

Peaches + Cream Pancakes

Serves 3 *(makes about 6 pancakes)*

There's nothing quite like a fluffy pancake for brunch! I like to make mine a bit fancier by pairing them with lightly charred peaches. Sheer perfection.

First, make the batter. In a large bowl, whisk together the dry ingredients. In another bowl whisk together the soya milk and lemon juice until thickened, then whisk in the vanilla bean paste and melted butter. Slowly pour the wet mixture into the dry mixture, whisking until just combined (see **NOTE**).

Add a drizzle of oil to a non-stick frying pan (skillet) set over a medium–high heat. Pat the peach slices dry with kitchen paper then place them into the pan in pairs, allowing plenty of space between each pair (work in batches). Allow the peach slices to cook for 1 minute then spoon a ladleful of batter on top of each pair. Cook the pancakes for 2–3 minutes, or until bubbles appear on the surface, then flip them and cook for a further 1 minute, or until golden brown on the other side. Keep the pancakes somewhere warm while you repeat the process with more peach slices and batter, to make 6 pancakes.

Place the whipping cream and vanilla bean paste in the bowl of a mixer (or use an electric hand whisk) and whisk until soft peaks form.

Serve up two pancakes on each plate, with a dollop of vanilla cream, a couple more peach slices and a drizzle of peach syrup. Scatter with chopped hazelnuts, if you like, then enjoy.

vegetable oil, for frying

400g (14oz) can peach slices in syrup (you'll need 18 slices), drained and syrup reserved

150ml (⅔ cup) vegan whipping cream

1 tsp vanilla bean paste

50g (1¾oz) toasted hazelnuts, chopped, to serve (optional)

FOR THE BATTER

250g (1¾ cup plus 2 tbsp) plain (all-purpose) flour

2 tbsp caster (superfine) sugar

2 tsp baking powder

½ tsp salt

240ml (1 cup) soya milk

1 tbsp lemon juice

1 tsp vanilla bean paste

40g (3 tbsp) vegan butter, melted

NOTE

My biggest tip here is to not overmix the pancake batter as you'll lose all that delicious fluffiness.

One Pan Full English

Serves 2

One-pan dishes were pretty much the only thing on regular rotation when I was a student. Minimal washing up and, if you're nursing a hangover, then they're a double win!

Set a large frying pan (skillet) over a medium heat and fry the sausages in the vegetable oil for 6 minutes. Next, add the bacon and tomatoes to the pan too and cook until the bacon is crispy, the tomatoes are blistered and the sausages are browned. Transfer everything to a plate and set aside.

Put the pan back over a high heat and add the mushrooms along with a pinch of salt. Cook them for about 5 minutes, stirring occasionally, until the water released from the mushrooms has cooked off and they are beginning to brown a little. Add the garlic, parsley and butter, and season well with salt and pepper, then stir and cook for a further 3 minutes.

Push the mushrooms to the side of the pan and add the crumbled firm tofu and spring onions. Season with salt and pepper then fry for about 2 minutes before adding all the remaining scramble ingredients (apart from the milk). Cook the scramble for about 3 minutes, breaking apart the silken tofu with a wooden spoon and mixing everything together until it's hot throughout. Taste the tofu and adjust the seasoning to your liking, then stir in the milk.

Push the scramble to the side of the pan then add the sausages, bacon and tomatoes back to the pan to warm through.

Serve in the middle of the table with toasted and buttered sourdough and brown sauce or ketchup on the side.

1 tbsp vegetable oil

4 vegan sausages

4 slices vegan bacon (I use La Vie)

125g (4½oz) cherry tomatoes on the vine

250g (9oz) small chestnut (cremini) mushrooms, halved or quartered

4 garlic cloves, minced

handful of parsley, roughly chopped

1 tbsp vegan butter, plus extra for buttering toast

2 slices sourdough bread, toasted

brown sauce or ketchup (optional), to serve

salt and freshly ground black pepper

FOR THE TOFU SCRAMBLE

140g (5oz) extra-firm tofu, drained and crumbled

2 spring onions (scallions), finely chopped

160g (5½oz) silken tofu, drained

2 sun dried tomatoes, finely chopped

small handful of chives, finely chopped

1 tbsp nutritional yeast

1 tbsp chilli jam or sweet chilli sauce

1 tsp smoked paprika

1 tsp dried mixed herbs

½ tsp ground cumin

3 tbsp dairy-free milk

Prep	Cook	Difficulty level	Protein per serving
5 mins	12 mins	1/5	11.8g (7/16oz)

Boozy Butter Beans + Greens

Serves 4

You've popped the prosecco already so it's a perfect day to do bottomless brunch at home! These gorgeous indulgent beans are done in under 20 minutes to give you more time to catch up with friends.

Add the olive oil to a pan set over a medium heat, then add the onion and leek and sauté for 5 minutes until golden. Deglaze the pan with the prosecco or white wine, then cook for 2 minutes more to allow the alcohol to cook off. Add the garlic and the butter beans, along with the liquid from the can, then season well with salt and pepper and stir.

Add the spinach, parsley, cheese, mustard and lemon juice then mix well. Taste and add a little more salt and pepper if needed, then cook for a few more minutes until gently bubbling.

Spread the toasted sourdough bread with some butter then top with your boozy beans. Finish with a drizzle of olive oil, some more vegan Parmesan and a sprinkle of chilli flakes.

1 tbsp olive oil, plus extra to drizzle

1 small onion, chopped

1 leek, chopped

3 garlic cloves, minced

400g (14oz) can good-quality butter (lima) beans (including the liquid from the can)

200ml (scant 1 cup) prosecco or white wine (ensure vegan)

200g (7oz) frozen spinach, defrosted and squeezed to remove excess water

handful of parsley, roughly chopped

75g (2½oz) vegan Parmesan, grated, plus extra to serve

½ tsp Dijon mustard

juice of ½ lemon

salt and freshly ground black pepper

TO SERVE

4 slices of sourdough bread, toasted

vegan butter

pinch of chilli (red pepper) flakes

Prep	Cook	Difficulty level	Protein per serving
10 mins	20–25 mins	2/5	20.6g (¾oz)

Breakfast Frittata

Serves 6

This is one of my go-to meal-prep recipes – it's done in half an hour but will feed you for the week. You can eat this chilled, warmed up on its own, or whack a slice in a bagel to create an "egg" sando.

Preheat your oven to 200°C (180°C fan/400°F/Gas 6).

Add a glug of oil to a medium-sized ovenproof frying pan (skillet) set over a medium–high heat. When hot, add the red pepper and onion and fry for 5 minutes until just starting to soften, then set aside.

Crumble the tofu into a food processor or blender and blitz until smooth. Scrape the blitzed tofu into a large bowl and add the softened red pepper and onion, spinach, sun dried tomatoes, hummus, chickpea flour, mustard, garlic powder, paprika and turmeric. Season well with salt and pepper then mix until combined.

Drizzle a little more oil into the frying pan and swirl to coat the base. Scrape the frittata mixture into the pan and use wet hands to press it down into a flat, even layer. Drizzle a little more oil on the top of the frittata then place it in the oven and bake for 20–25 minutes until firm.

When cooked, allow to rest for at least 10 minutes, then serve in slices with dollops of yogurt, a sprinkling of chives, chilli flakes and kala namak (optional), and lemon wedges for squeezing.

1 red (bell) pepper, diced

1 red onion, sliced

600g (21oz) medium-firm tofu, drained

150g (5½oz) frozen spinach, thawed then squeezed to remove excess water

9 sun dried tomatoes, chopped

4½ tbsp hummus

3 tbsp chickpea (gram) flour

1½ tsp Dijon mustard

1½ tsp garlic powder

1½ tsp smoked paprika

pinch of ground turmeric

salt and freshly ground black pepper

TO SERVE

small handful of chives, finely chopped

dried chilli (red pepper) flakes

kala namak (optional; page 13)

6 tbsp vegan yogurt

lemon wedges, for squeezing

Prep	Cook	Difficulty level	Protein per serving
5 mins	30 mins	1/5	14.8g (½oz)

Smoky Sausage Mockmuffins

Makes 6

There is a café chain (who shall not be named) whose vegan breakfast muffin had me in a chokehold for a loooong time… until I made this. When I have these ready to go in the fridge, I feel like every element of my life is just a little bit more put together. Make them, stock up and thank me later!

Combine all the smoky tomato sauce ingredients in a saucepan, crushing the tomatoes with your hands or a spoon as you add them. Set over a low-medium heat, bring to a simmer, then simmer for 30 minutes, stirring occasionally, until reduced and thickened. Taste for seasoning, adding more salt and pepper if needed.

Meanwhile, add the white beans to a large bowl and crush them using your hands or a potato masher. Add the remaining patty ingredients and mix until very well combined (it's useful to use your hands here). Split the patty mixture into 6 equal balls, then squash them into burger patty shapes.

Add a drizzle of oil to a frying pan (skillet) set over a medium heat. Add the patties to the pan in batches, cooking them for 3 minutes on each side until golden brown.

Spread a dollop of smoky tomato sauce on the muffin bottoms, then top each with a sausage patty and a slice of cheese. Add the muffin tops and serve. Alternatively, wrap the muffins in foil and store in the fridge for 5 days or the freezer for 3 months. To reheat, allow them to defrost fully in the fridge if frozen, then simply pop them in the oven (foil still in place) at 200°C (180°C fan/400°F/Gas 6) for 5 minutes.

vegetable oil, for frying

6 English muffins, split and toasted

6 slices meltable vegan Cheddar

FOR THE PATTY

400g (14oz) can white beans, drained and rinsed

8 vegan sausages (the "meaty" type), skins removed

200g (7oz) frozen spinach, thawed and squeezed of excess water, then finely chopped

small handful of chives, finely chopped

30g (scant ⅓ cup) fine golden breadcrumbs

1 tbsp dried mixed herbs

1 tsp ground fennel seeds

1 tsp garlic powder

1 tsp freshly ground black pepper

½ tsp salt

FOR THE SMOKY TOMATO SAUCE

400g (14oz) can plum tomatoes

1 tbsp balsamic vinegar

2 tsp smoked paprika

1 tsp caster (superfine) sugar

½ tsp salt

pinch of freshly ground black pepper

NOTE

If storing wrapped in the fridge, keep them upside down to avoid the tomato sauce making the muffin base soggy.

Prep	Cook	Difficulty level	Protein per serving
5 mins	10 mins	2/5	1: 31.4g (1oz)
			2: 30.8g (1oz)

Rice Paper Omelette

Serves 2 *(per variation)*

Prep this mix ahead of time for a super-speedy midweek breakfast when you need that omelette fix. The kala namak is optional but will give you the extra "eggy" taste that really ties the whole thing together.

Begin by adding all the "egg" base ingredients to a high speed blender, along with a pinch each of black pepper and kala namak (optional – you can use normal salt instead). Blitz until smooth – the consistency should be thick, like hummus.

For a cheesy pesto omelette [1]

Place a lidded frying pan (skillet) over medium–low heat and add ½ tablespoon of olive oil and 1 tablespoon of pesto. Allow them to melt together, then tilt and swirl the pan to coat the base. Place one sheet of rice paper into the pan then spoon over half the "egg" base mixture, spreading it out evenly over the rice paper. Reduce the heat to low, pop the lid on and cook for 5 minutes.

Sprinkle over half the cheese and dot with an extra ½ tablespoon of pesto, then season with a little black salt and scatter with a few chopped chives and basil leaves. Using a spatula, gently fold the omelette in half to melt the cheese, then slide onto a plate to serve. Repeat to make a second omelette. Season and serve.

For a loaded + spicy omelette [2]

Place a lidded frying pan (skillet) over medium–low heat and add a sheet of rice paper to the dry pan. Drizzle 1 teaspoon of chilli oil on top and spread it evenly (a silicone pastry brush is useful here). Spoon over half the "egg" base mixture, spreading it out evenly over the rice paper. Scatter over half the spring onions and coriander, then reduce the heat to low, pop the lid on and cook for 5 minutes.

Sprinkle over half the cheese then replace the lid and cook for 1 minute to melt the cheese. Without folding the omelette, slide it out onto a plate. Cover the omelette with sriracha, sesame seeds and/or crispy onions (I like to use everything!) then season and serve. Repeat to make a second omelette.

FOR THE "EGG" BASE

240g (8½oz) extra-firm tofu, drained

160g (5½oz) silken tofu, drained

4 tbsp dairy-free milk

4 tbsp chickpea (gram) flour

3 tbsp nutritional yeast

2 tbsp cornflour (cornstarch)

1 tsp baking powder

1 tsp garlic powder

1 tsp smoked paprika

½ tsp ground turmeric

kala namak (optional; page 13)

salt and freshly ground black pepper

FOR A CHEESY PESTO OMELETTE

1 tbsp olive oil

3 tbsp vegan pesto

2 sheets rice paper

80g (3oz) meltable vegan Cheddar, grated

basil and chopped chives, to serve

FOR A LOADED + SPICY OMELETTE

2 sheets rice paper

2 tsp chilli oil

2 spring onions (scallions), chopped

small handful of coriander (cilantro), roughly chopped

50g (1¾oz) meltable vegan Cheddar, grated

sriracha, to serve

sesame seeds and/or crispy onions, to serve

Prep	Cook	Difficulty level	Protein per serving
5 mins	0 mins	1/5	20.8g (¾oz)

Chocolate Protein Pots

Serves 2

Who doesn't want to feel like they're eating chocolate pudding for breakfast? These little pots are one of the easiest things in this book to prep and will keep you full all morning.

Melt the chocolate in a small heatproof bowl set over a saucepan or in the microwave in 20 second bursts.

Add the remaining ingredients to a blender or food processor and pour in the melted chocolate. Blitz until completely smooth.

Scrape the mixture equally between two bowls or glasses. You can either cover and refrigerate until needed or eat it straight away.

When ready to serve, top the chocolate pots with a handful of granola and your choice of fresh berries.

70g (2½oz) dark chocolate (ensure vegan)

300g (10½oz) silken tofu, drained

2 tbsp almond or peanut butter

2 tbsp agave syrup

2 tbsp chia seeds

1 tbsp unsweetened cocoa powder

½ tsp vanilla extract

pinch of salt

TO SERVE

handful of granola

fresh berries of your choice

2

Small
Plates

It's time to elevate your dinner parties and jazz up those weeknight suppers.

Sticky Pomegranate Aubergine

44

Lemon Pepper Mushroom Wings

46

Crispy Spiced Filo Rolls

48

Nutty Smashed Cucumbers

51

Miso + Lemon Broccoli

52

Cheesy Kale

54

Sweet Chilli Carrots

56

Garlic Parm Roasties

61

Squash Croquettes

62

Thai-style Fish Cakes

65

Sticky Pomegranate Aubergine

Serves 4 *(as a side)*

I know some people have a love/hate relationship with aubergine, but I'm hoping this will change the haters' minds. Any sweet and sticky sauce is a winner in my book and this pomegranate glaze is utter perfection. I love to eat this with rice for supper, but it's also great as a side served with the tahini yogurt.

Lightly salt the aubergine slices on both sides then lay them on a sheet or two of kitchen paper. Cover with more kitchen paper and leave to one side for 5 minutes to allow moisture to be drawn out of the aubergine.

Mix together the yogurt, tahini and lemon juice in a small bowl. Season generously with salt and pepper and refrigerate until ready to serve.

Place the pomegranate juice, tamari, sugar and garlic in a small saucepan and set it over a medium heat. Simmer for about 5 minutes, or until the mixture has reduced by about half and you have a thickened glaze.

Remove the aubergine slices from the kitchen paper and pat dry, then dust on both sides with the cornflour.

Set a large frying pan (skillet) over a medium-high and drizzle in the olive oil. Once hot, fry the aubergine for about 5 minutes on each side, until the slices are a deep golden-brown all over. Add about three-quarters of the pomegranate glaze to the aubergine pan and stir to coat until each slice is glossy.

Spread the tahini yogurt on a plate and top with the aubergine. Drizzle over the remaining glaze and finish with pomegranate seeds and some mint leaves. Serve immediately.

1 aubergine (eggplant), sliced into about 1cm (½in) rounds

140g (generous ½ cup) dairy-free yogurt

2 tbsp tahini (sesame paste)

juice of ½ lemon

160ml (generous ⅔ cup) pomegranate juice

1 tbsp tamari or light soy sauce

2 tsp soft light brown sugar

1 garlic clove, minced

1½ tbsp cornflour (cornstarch)

2 tbsp olive oil

handful of pomegranate seeds, to serve

small handful of mint leaves (optional)

salt and freshly ground black pepper

NOTE

Don't skip salting the aubergine flesh – it draws out the bitterness and reduces oil absorption.

Prep	Cook	Difficulty level	Protein per serving
10 mins	30 mins	2/5	7.1g (¼oz)

Lemon Pepper Mushroom Wings

Serves 3

These are just as good served with a herby salad for dinner, as they are shared with friends and beers. But you may want to double the recipe in that case, as these disappear quickly!

Preheat your oven to 220°C (200°C fan/425°F/Gas 7) and line a baking sheet with baking parchment. Alternatively, preheat your air fryer to 190°C (375°F) and spray or drizzle the basket with the oil.

Grab 3 deep bowls: place the flour, garlic powder and half the lemon zest into one bowl; add the soya milk and cornflour to another bowl; then add the breadcrumbs, black pepper, salt, oregano and the remaining lemon zest to the final bowl. Stir each bowl well.

If your oyster mushrooms are in clusters or very large, tear them apart into individual or smaller even-sized pieces. Working in batches, place the mushrooms into the flour bowl and toss to fully coat. Next, add them to the milk and cornflour bowl and stir to coat. Finally place them into the breadcrumb bowl and toss to coat once again – you may need to pat the breadcrumbs onto the mushrooms to coat them fully. Repeat until you have coated all of your mushrooms.

Place the mushrooms on the lined baking sheet or in the greased air fryer basket and spray or drizzle with a little oil. Cook in the oven or air fryer for 25–30 minutes, flipping the mushrooms halfway through to ensure they are fully golden and crisp.

While the mushrooms are cooking, add all the ingredients for the lemon mustard mayo to a bowl, reserving some of the parsley to serve, and mix well. Taste and add salt and pepper as needed.

Sprinkle the cooked mushrooms with a pinch of salt and the reserved parsley. Serve immediately with lemon wedges on the side for squeezing and the lemon mustard mayo for dipping.

vegetable oil, for drizzling/spraying

2 tbsp plain (all-purpose) flour

1 tsp garlic powder

zest of 1 lemon

100ml (6½ tbsp) soya milk

1 tbsp cornflour (cornstarch)

70g (1¾ cups) panko breadcrumbs

1 tsp freshly ground black pepper, plus extra for seasoning

½ tsp salt, plus extra for seasoning

1 tsp dried oregano

150g (5½oz) oyster mushrooms

FOR THE LEMON MUSTARD MAYO

3 tbsp vegan mayo

a few sprigs of parsley, leaves picked and finely chopped

1 tsp wholegrain mustard

juice of ¼ lemon, remaining lemon cut into wedges to serve

NOTE

Like most things, these can also be deep-fried and will go even more golden and crispy!
If deep-frying they will only take 2 minutes to cook.

Prep	Cook	Difficulty level	Protein per roll
10 mins	12–14 mins	2/5	4.5g (³⁄₁₆oz)

Crispy Spiced Filo Rolls

Makes 12

My version of a grown-up sausage roll, these delicious bites are always a crowd-pleaser. The crunch, the spicy mince and the cooling yogurt... gimme all 12!

Preheat the oven to 220°C (200°C fan/425°F/Gas 7) and line a baking sheet with baking parchment.

To make the filling, place the grated onion in a small bowl along with the lemon juice and a generous pinch of salt. Allow it to sit for a couple of minutes, then use your hands to squeeze out as much liquid as possible. Transfer the onion to a large bowl along with the remaining filling ingredients and mix well.

Lay a sheet of filo pastry on a clean surface, brush it with a little olive oil, then place another sheet on top. Place half the filling mixture in a line along the long side of the pastry and compact the mixture into a log shape with your hands. Roll up the pastry to conceal the filling, then brush it all over with a little more olive oil and cut it into six equal pieces. Repeat with the remaining pastry and filling to give you 12 rolls.

Sprinkle sesame seeds all over each roll, then transfer them to your lined baking sheet and bake for 12–14 minutes until golden and crisp.

Mix together all the ingredients for the cumin yogurt in a small bowl then serve it alongside your crispy spiced filo rolls for dipping.

4 sheets of filo (phyllo) pastry (ensure vegan)

olive oil, for brushing

mixed sesame seeds, for sprinkling

salt and freshly ground black pepper

FOR THE FILLING

1 onion, coarsely grated

juice of ½ lemon

200g (7oz) vegan mince (vegan ground meat)

small handful of mint, leaves picked and finely chopped

small handful of flat-leaf parsley, finely chopped

3 garlic cloves, minced

1½ tbsp ras el hanout

1 tbsp olive oil

1 tbsp tomato purée (paste)

1 tbsp balsamic vinegar

FOR THE CUMIN YOGURT

3 tbsp vegan yogurt

1 tsp ground cumin

½ tsp garlic powder

squeeze of lemon juice

Prep	Marinate	Difficulty level	Protein per serving
5 mins	30 mins	1/5	6.3g (¼oz)

Nutty Smashed Cucumbers

Serves 3 *(as a side)*

If I have a cucumber in the fridge, I will never not make this recipe. I've even forgotten what plain cucumber tastes like, it's just that good! It's super quick to whip up and it gets tastier the longer the cucumber soaks in that gorgeous umami marinade.

Combine all the marinade ingredients in a large bowl and whisk until smooth. The marinade should be the consistency of a thick batter; if it's too thick, add a little more hot water.

Using a rolling pin or tenderizer, bash the cucumber firmly so that it bruises and splits in places (doing this allows the marinade to cling to the cucumber more easily than if you'd simply sliced it). Once smashed, chop the cucumber into roughly 1 cm (½in) pieces, add it to the bowl with the marinade and mix well to coat.

You can eat this straight away but I'd recommend marinating it in the fridge for a minimum of 30 minutes (overnight is best) to allow the flavours to develop. To serve, drizzle with a little more chilli oil and sprinkle with sesame seeds.

1 large cucumber

sesame seeds, to serve

FOR THE MARINADE

3½ tbsp smooth peanut butter

1 tbsp dark soy sauce

1 tbsp mirin

1 tsp chilli oil, plus extra to serve

1 garlic clove, minced

1cm (½in) piece of fresh root ginger, minced

juice of 1 lime

1 tbsp hot water, plus extra if needed

pinch of salt

Miso + Lemon Broccoli *with* Whipped Spring Onion Tofu

Serves 2 *(as a side)*

Is it controversial for broccoli to be your fave vegetable? I don't think so. I swear I could eat this particular dish for every meal of the day and not get bored. The miso adds a delicious umami flavour and makes this even more addictive.

Preheat the oven to 190°C (170°C fan/375°F/Gas 5) and line a baking tray (sheet) with baking parchment.

In a bowl large enough to fit the broccoli, add the olive oil, miso paste, maple syrup, garlic, nutritional yeast and lemon zest and juice, then mix well until smooth. Add the broccoli and toss well, ensuring each floret is coated in the dressing.

Tip the broccoli onto the lined baking tray and cover with foil, then bake for 14–18 minutes, removing the foil half way through cooking, until tender (check by piercing the stems with a sharp knife).

To make the whipped spring onion tofu, simply add all the ingredients to a blender or food processor and blitz until smooth. Taste, then season with salt and pepper.

Dollop and spread the whipped tofu onto a platter then top with the broccoli. Drizzle with chilli oil and serve immediately.

160g (5¾oz) tenderstem broccoli

1 tbsp olive oil

1 tbsp white miso paste

1 tsp maple syrup

1 garlic clove, minced

1 tbsp nutritional yeast

zest and juice of ½ lemon

chilli oil, to serve

salt and freshly ground black pepper

FOR WHIPPED SPRING ONION TOFU

150g (5½oz) silken tofu

2 spring onions (scallions), roughly chopped

zest and juice of ½ lemon

1 tbsp nutritional yeast

½ tsp garlic powder

Prep	Cook	Difficulty level	Protein per serving
2 mins	4 mins	1/5	3.1g (⅛oz)

Cheesy Kale

Serves 4 *(as a side)*

This recipe fully converted my veg-averse family so, if you're looking for ways to add more leafy greens to your diet, give this a whirl. The vinegar may seem odd, but it adds an element of tanginess to the nutritional yeast that makes the finished dish taste really "cheesy".

1 tbsp olive oil

200g (7oz) cavolo nero (lacinato kale) or curly kale, tough stems removed and leaves cut into 2.5cm (1in) pieces

1 garlic clove, minced

½ tsp salt

pinch of nutmeg

2 tbsp nutritional yeast

1½ tsp apple cider vinegar

30g (1oz) crispy onions, to serve

Set a lidded frying pan (skillet) over a medium–low heat and add the olive oil. When hot, add the kale, garlic and salt and fry for about 3 minutes, uncovered, until the kale begins to soften.

Add the remaining ingredients to the pan (except the crispy onions) and stir well, then place the lid on the pan to allow the kale to steam for a final 1 minute.

Serve immediately with crispy onions on top.

Prep	Cook	Difficulty level	Protein per serving
5 mins	40–45 mins	2/5	4.7g (³⁄₁₆oz)

Sweet Chilli Carrots

Serves 6 *(as a side)*

Sticky, spicy and sweet, these carrots are addictive when paired with a creamy tangy yogurt – you'll never return to regular roast carrots after you've tried them!

Preheat your oven to 200°C (180°C fan/400°F/Gas 6).

Place the carrots in a baking dish along with the olive oil, paprika, garlic powder, cumin and some salt and pepper. Toss well then roast for 30–35 minutes until tender.

Add the thyme leaves, sweet chilli sauce and soy sauce to the carrots, mix thoroughly, then return to the oven for a further 10 minutes.

Meanwhile, crumble the feta into the yogurt, season well with salt and pepper and stir to combine.

Spoon and spread the yogurt on a large serving plate, then top with the carrots. Dot over a little more sweet chilli sauce or chilli jam, then scatter over some more crumbled feta and thyme leaves before serving.

500g (1lb 2oz) Chantenay carrots (or other baby carrots)

1 tbsp olive oil

1 tsp smoked paprika

½ tsp garlic powder

½ tsp ground cumin

1 tbsp sweet chilli sauce or chilli jam, plus extra to serve

1 tbsp light soy sauce

a few sprigs of thyme, leaves stripped, plus extra to serve

400g (14oz) thick Greek-style vegan yogurt

50g (1¾oz) vegan feta, plus extra to serve

salt and freshly ground black pepper

Prep	Cook	Difficulty level	Protein per serving
5 mins	45–50 mins	2/5	9.8g (⅜oz)

Garlic Parm Roasties

Serves 4 *(as a side)*

Three of my favourite things: cheese, garlic and potatoes. I usually double the batch of cashew Parm so I can keep half in the fridge for sprinkling over pasta dishes.

Preheat your oven to 220°C (200°C fan/425°F/Gas 7). Add the oil to a deep baking tray and place in the oven to get hot.

Place the potatoes into a large saucepan of cold, salted water and bring to the boil. Boil for 8–10 minutes before draining and leaving to steam dry.

Meanwhile, make the cashew Parm. Add the cashew nuts, nutritional yeast, garlic powder and 1 teaspoon of salt to a food processor or blender and blitz to a fine crumb.

Add the potatoes to a large bowl along with half the cashew Parm. Place a plate on top of the bowl, hold tightly and shake to ruffle the potatoes. If there is any cashew Parm left in the bowl after shaking, press it onto the potatoes with your hands.

Remove the baking tray from the oven and carefully place the potatoes into the hot oil. Return the tray to the oven and bake for 35–40 minutes, turning each potato halfway through, until they are evenly golden and crispy.

Pile the potatoes into a serving bowl, season with some salt and pepper, then top with the remaining cashew Parm and sprinkle with some parsley.

4 tbsp vegetable oil

4 large maris piper potatoes, peeled and cut into 5cm (2in) pieces

handful of parsley, roughly chopped

salt and freshly ground black pepper

FOR THE CASHEW PARM

75g (2½oz) cashew nuts

3 tbsp nutritional yeast

½ tsp garlic powder

NOTE

Make sure you whizz the cashew Parm up super fine so it sticks to the potatoes properly. This will help you achieve the crispy edges that make an excellent roast potato.

Prep	Cook	Difficulty level	Protein per serving
30 mins (+ chilling)	1 hour	3/5	6g (¼oz)

Squash Croquettes *with* Harissa Crème

Serves 6 *(as a snack)*

A sophisticated twist on the comforting classic. The coconut in the crumb brings out the sweetness of the squash, and paired with the spicy dip makes these hard to put down!

Preheat your oven to 220°C (200°C fan/425°F/Gas 7).

Place the squash halves cut-side up in a baking dish, drizzle with the olive oil and season with salt and pepper. Roast for 35–40 minutes, or until the flesh is soft. Once cooked, allow to cool fully. Scoop the cooled squash flesh into a large bowl and mash with a fork until smooth. Add the shallot, feta, fresh herbs, chickpea flour, garlic, cumin, cayenne pepper and salt and pepper, then stir well. The mixture should feel mouldable – if it feels a little too wet mix in some more chickpea flour. Roll the mixture into 16 equal balls.

Grab 3 bowls: place the plain flour into one bowl; mix the soya milk, lemon juice and a pinch of cayenne pepper in another bowl; then mix the breadcrumbs and desiccated coconut in the final bowl. Dredge each ball in the plain flour, then in the wet mixture, then toss in the breadcrumb and coconut mixture, ensuring they're coated all over. Transfer to a plate and refrigerate for 10–15 minutes.

Meanwhile, make the harissa crème by mixing all the ingredients together in a bowl. Season to taste with salt and pepper.

Heat the vegetable oil in a deep-sided saucepan set over a medium heat, ensuring the oil comes no more than two-thirds up the side of the pan. Once hot (test by adding a pinch of breadcrumbs – if they sizzle and turn golden in 30 seconds the oil is ready), fry the croquettes in batches for 3–4 minutes until golden and crispy. Using a slotted spoon, transfer the croquettes to a plate lined with kitchen paper.

Serve the croquettes alongside the harissa crème for dipping.

1 small butternut squash, halved and seeds removed

½ tbsp olive oil

1 shallot, finely chopped

50g (1¾oz) vegan feta, finely crumbled

small handful of parsley, chopped

small handful of chives, chopped

50g (6 tbsp) chickpea (gram) flour

1 garlic clove, minced

1 tsp ground cumin

½ tsp ground cayenne pepper, plus a pinch

50g (6 tbsp) plain (all-purpose) flour

100ml (6½ tbsp) soya milk

juice ½ lemon

50g (generous 1 cup) panko breadcrumbs

50g (¾ cup) desiccated (dried shredded) coconut

500ml (generous 2 cups) vegetable oil, for deep frying

FOR THE HARISSA CRÈME

200g (7oz) vegan crème fraîche

1 tbsp harissa paste

zest of 1 lemon

1 garlic clove, minced

NOTE

You can also cook these in your air fryer. They might not be as golden but they will still be delicious. Spray all over with oil, then air fry at 200°C (400°F) for 10–12 minutes.

Prep	Cook	Difficulty level	Protein per fish cake
15 mins	30 mins	3/5	5.6g (³⁄₁₆oz)

Thai-Style Fish Cakes

Makes 10

Fish cakes were a staple during my uni days, so I like to think of myself as a bit of a connoisseur... I've attempted so many different texture, flavour and nutrition combinations while trying to recreate a perfect vegan alternative and these are the reigning champs. The secret is jackfruit for flakiness and chickpeas for protein. You can store these in the freezer then simply reheat them in the oven for the speediest, most delicious lunch, or to share with your friends. Try serving them with my nutty smashed cucumbers (page 51) or as part of a snacky spread with sweet chilli sauce for dipping.

Preheat your oven to 220°C (200°C fan/425°F/Gas 7) and line a baking sheet with baking parchment. Alternatively, preheat your air fryer to 200°C (400°F) and spray or drizzle the basket with oil.

Boil the potato in a pan of boiling water for 12–14 minutes until you can pierce it with a knife without resistance. Drain then pat dry.

Place the jackfruit into a clean kitchen towel and squeeze it over the sink to remove any excess liquid. Remove any hard stems and seeds, then add it to a mixing bowl along with the chickpeas and cooked potato. Mash everything together well.

Add the spring onions, curry paste, fish sauce, nori and lime zest and season with salt and pepper (go easy on the salt; the fish sauce and nori are already salty). Mix again so everything is combined then add the breadcrumbs and flour and mix for a final time. Form the mixture into 10 equal patties then drizzle each with a little vegetable oil.

Add the sesame seeds to a shallow bowl, then dip each of the patties into them to coat. Place the patties on the lined baking sheet or in the greased air fryer basket and cook for 10–15 minutes, carefully flipping them halfway, until golden on both sides. Alternatively, you can shallow fry them in a little oil in a frying pan (skillet) set over a low heat for 8–10 minutes, flipping as needed until golden.

vegetable oil, for drizzling/spraying

1 large baking potato (about 200g/7oz), peeled and cubed

400g (14oz) can jackfruit, drained

400g (14oz) can chickpeas, drained and rinsed

3 spring onions (scallions), finely chopped

3 tbsp vegan red Thai curry paste

1 tbsp vegan fish sauce (or use light soy sauce)

2 sheets nori, crumbled into very small pieces

zest of ½ lime

50g (½ cup) fine golden breadcrumbs

2 tbsp plain (all-purpose) flour

100g (¾ cup) black and white sesame seeds

salt and freshly ground black pepper

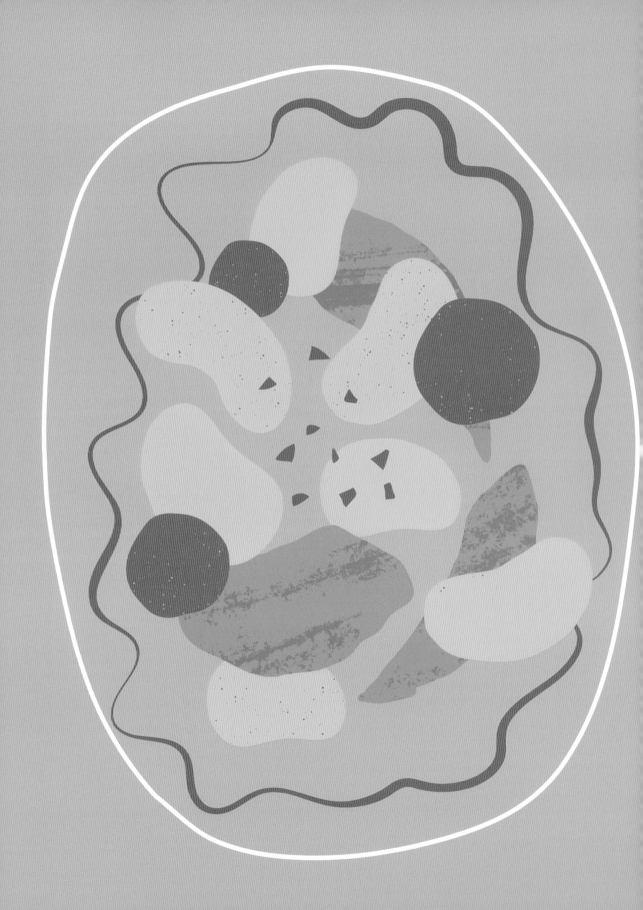

3

Quick
Plates

Whether you need food in a flash, or have a good half-hour to spare, this chapter is your go-to for busy weekdays, with recipes flowing from speediest to slowest (but all still under 30 minutes!).

Kimchi Beans

70

Caesar Chickpea Pitta Pockets

72

Hummus Pasta

74

'Nduja Flatbreads

77

Coconut Tofu *with* Spicy Mango Sauce

78

Mushroom + Jackfruit Chimichurri Tacos

80

Crispy Gnocchi *with* Romesco Hummus

82

Cannellini, Cheese + Chive Tarts

84

Gochujang + Black Bean Loaded Sweet Potatoes

89

Kimchi Beans

Serves 3

I'm not a beans-on-toast girl unless I can make it from scratch. These beans are full of gut goodness from the fermented kimchi and loads of fibre from the beans. They're perfect as a spicy breakfast option, WFH lunch or when you can't be bothered with dinner – the people's princess of the bean world.

Add a glug of olive oil to a pan set over a medium heat. When hot, add the shallots or spring onions, ginger and garlic and sauté for 5 minutes until fragrant. Stir in the peppers, tomato purée and gochujang paste and cook for a further minute, then add the kimchi and butter beans along with all the liquid from the jar.

Stir well and cook until simmering, then add the cheese, nutritional yeast and coriander (if using). Cook and stir until the cheese has melted then season well with salt and pepper. Spoon the beans onto your sourdough toast and finish with a dollop of yogurt, a drizzle of chilli oil and some dill sprinkled over.

glug of olive oil

2 shallots or spring onions (scallions), finely chopped

1 garlic clove, minced

2.5cm (1in) piece of fresh root ginger, minced

100g (3½oz) roasted red (bell) peppers (the kind from a jar), roughly chopped

1 tbsp tomato purée (paste)

1 tbsp gochujang paste

250g (9oz) kimchi, roughly chopped

570g (1¼lb) jar butter (lima) beans (including the liquid from the jar)

60g (2oz) meltable vegan Cheddar, grated

2 tbsp nutritional yeast

small handful of coriander (cilantro), chopped (optional)

salt and freshly ground black pepper

TO SERVE

6 slices sourdough bread, toasted

3 tbsp vegan yogurt

chilli oil

small handful of dill, roughly chopped

Caesar Chickpea Pitta Pockets

Serves 2

Caesar is my number one dressing, and it's surprisingly very straightforward to make vegan. The chickpeas give the same satisfying crunch as a crouton and a great protein boost too.

Preheat your oven to 210°C (190°C fan/410°F/Gas 6–7) and line a baking sheet with baking parchment. Alternatively, preheat your air fryer to 190°C (375°F) and spray or drizzle the basket with oil.

If your chickpeas are still wet, pat them dry using kitchen paper. In a large bowl, combine the chickpeas with olive oil, oregano and some salt and pepper then tip them onto your lined baking sheet or into your air fryer basket. Bake for 12 minutes in the oven or 8 minutes in the air fryer, stirring them halfway through, until golden and starting to crisp.

For the dressing, simply mix all the ingredients together in a small bowl until well combined. Taste and season with salt and pepper.

Toast the pittas then slice along the long edge of each one to open them up. Into each pitta pocket drizzle some dressing, add half the lettuce and tomato, then top with half the chickpeas and drizzle with more dressing before tucking in.

400g (14oz) can chickpeas, drained and rinsed

1 tbsp olive oil, plus extra for greasing

1 tsp dried oregano

2 pitta breads

1 Little Gem lettuce, roughly chopped

1 medium tomato, diced

salt and freshly ground black pepper

FOR THE DRESSING

3 tbsp vegan mayo

juice of ½ lemon

1 tsp vegan Worcestershire sauce

½ tsp Dijon mustard

1 tbsp nutritional yeast

2 cornichons, finely chopped

1 tbsp capers, finely chopped

1 garlic clove, minced

Hummus Pasta

Serves 2

This is the ultimate fridge clear-out dish for when you've run out of fresh vegetables but have a million jars sitting on your top shelf. Try experimenting with different hummus – I love using jalapeño hummus for an extra kick of heat.

Cook the pasta in heavily salted water according to the packet instructions until al dente. Drain, reserving a mugful of the pasta cooking water.

Add the pasta back to the pan along with all the remaining ingredients and stir to combine, adding a splash of pasta cooking water to loosen the sauce a little. Place the pan back over a low heat for a couple of minutes to ensure everything is hot, then season well with salt and pepper before serving.

175g (6oz) gemelli pasta, or shape of your choice (ensure vegan)

6½ tbsp store-bought hummus

about 15 pitted green olives, drained and roughly chopped

about 6 sun dried tomatoes in oil, drained and roughly chopped

about 6 cooked artichoke hearts in oil, drained and roughly chopped

handful of parsley, roughly chopped

juice of ½ lemon

pinch of dried chilli (red pepper) flakes

drizzle of olive oil

salt and freshly ground black pepper

Prep	Cook	Difficulty level	Protein per serving
5 mins	15 mins	2/5	7g (¼oz)

'Nduja Flatbreads

Serves 6

A few years ago, 'nduja had a real moment in the food world and I felt a bit left out. So, I decided to recreate a plant-based version of this traditional spicy sausage paste from the Calabria region in Italy. One day, I finally cracked the code for the perfect vegan alternative. It can be tricky to find Calabrian chillies – I've made this with regular red chillies and Calabrian chilli paste and it works well with either.

First make the 'nduja. Add the olive oil to a non-stick frying pan (skillet) set over a medium heat.

Using a sharp knife, lightly score a line down the length of each sausage then peel away and discard the skin. Add the sausages to the hot pan and use a wooden spoon to break them apart. Fry the sausages for 5 minutes, squashing and breaking them apart with the spoon as they cook to achieve a crumbly texture.

Add the chopped chillies and fry for a further minute until fragrant, then stir in the tomato purée, paprika and cayenne and season lightly with salt and pepper. Deglaze the pan with the balsamic vinegar then remove the pan from the heat and leave to cool slightly.

Transfer the sausage mixture to a food processor, along with the sun dried tomatoes and 2 tablespoons of oil from the jar. Blitz to a paste (a few chunks is fine) then taste and add salt and pepper if needed.

Preheat your grill (broiler) to high.

Divide the 'nduja mixture between the six flatbreads and spread it out evenly. Add a few slices of tomato and onion to each then place under the hot grill for 3–5 minutes until the edges of the bread and the onions are lightly browned. Top with some basil and a dollop of mayo.

6 store-bought flatbreads (ensure vegan)

2 beef tomatoes, thinly sliced

1 small red onion, thinly sliced

small handful of basil, leaves picked and roughly torn

2 tbsp vegan mayo

salt and freshly ground black pepper

FOR THE 'NDUJA

1 tbsp olive oil

6 vegan sausages (the "meaty" type)

2 red chillies, deseeded and finely chopped, or 1 tbsp Calabrian chilli paste

2 tbsp tomato purée (paste)

1 tbsp smoked paprika

½ tsp ground cayenne pepper

2 tbsp balsamic vinegar

12 sun dried tomatoes, plus 2 tbsp oil from the jar

Prep	Cook	Difficulty level	Protein per serving
5 mins	12–16 mins	3/5	32.6g (1¼oz)

Coconut Tofu *with* Spicy Mango Sauce

Serves 2

This is my ultimate late night post-workout meal. It's so easy to make and the edamame are the perfect protein boost for a tired body. I love to use desiccated coconut instead of breadcrumbs sometimes when making crispy tofu – try it and see what you think!

Preheat your oven to 210°C (190°C fan/410°F/Gas 6–7) and line a baking sheet with baking parchment. Alternatively, preheat your air fryer to 190°C (375°F) and spray or drizzle the basket with vegetable oil.

Meanwhile, combine the desiccated coconut, paprika, garam masala, turmeric and some salt and pepper in a bowl. In another bowl mix the cornflour with 2 tablespoons of water to make a slurry.

Toss the tofu in the cornflour slurry then immediately add it to the coconut mixture, tossing to coat and pressing the coconut onto the tofu with your fingers. Drizzle the coated tofu with a little oil then tip out onto your lined baking sheet or into the air fryer basket. Bake in the oven for 16 minutes or in the air fryer for 12 minutes, tossing occasionally, until crispy and golden.

Microwave the rice according to the packet instructions.

Combine the ingredients for the spicy mango sauce in a small bowl.

Divide the rice between bowls and top with the crispy coconut tofu, some avocado and edamame beans. Spoon over the spicy mango sauce and serve with some chilli flakes sprinkled over.

vegetable oil, for drizzling/greasing

5 tbsp desiccated (dried shredded) coconut

1 tsp smoked paprika

½ tsp garam masala

½ tsp ground turmeric

2 tbsp cornflour (cornstarch)

225g (8oz) extra-firm tofu, drained and roughly torn into cubes

1 pouch (about 220g/8oz) microwavable rice

1 avocado, halved, pitted and sliced

150g (5½oz) edamame beans

dried chilli (red pepper) flakes, to serve (optional)

salt and freshly ground black pepper

FOR THE SPICY MANGO SAUCE

2 tbsp mango chutney

juice of ½ lime

1 tbsp sriracha

1 tbsp light soy sauce

½ tbsp chilli oil

Mushroom + Jackfruit Chimichurri Tacos

Serves 2–4 *(depending on hunger levels!)*

This zingy chimichurri is SO good – I would bathe in it if I could – and it's the secret behind these flavour-packed tacos. With the added texture of pulled oyster mushrooms and jackfruit, this recipe is one of my favourites when I'm craving something nourishing but still super-satisfying.

For the chimichurri, simply combine all ingredients together in a bowl and season with salt and pepper. Set aside.

Preheat the oven to 240°C (220°C fan/475°F/Gas 9) and line a baking sheet with baking parchment.

Place the jackfruit in a clean tea towel or cloth and squeeze it above the sink to remove as much liquid as possible. Discard any hard stems and seeds then transfer it to the lined baking sheet along with the mushrooms.

Add the olive oil, garlic, dried mixed herbs and ½ teaspoon each of salt and pepper to the jackfruit and mushrooms then toss together. Bake for 15 minutes, stirring halfway through, then stir through the black beans and return to the oven for 2–3 minutes to warm through. At the same time, add the mini tortillas to the rack below to warm those too.

Load your warm tortillas with some avocado and the jackfruit and mushroom mixture, then drizzle over the chimichurri and top with pickled red onions and a dusting of paprika.

8 mini tortillas

1 avocado, halved, pitted and sliced

store-bought pickled red onions

pinch of smoked paprika

salt and freshly ground black pepper

FOR THE CHIMICHURRI

handful of parsley, finely chopped

small handful of mint sprigs, leaves picked and finely chopped

½ red chilli, finely chopped

1 garlic clove, minced

1 tsp dried oregano

1 tbsp red wine vinegar

2 tbsp olive oil

FOR THE MUSHROOM + JACKFRUIT

500g (1lb 2oz) can jackfruit, drained

250g (9oz) chestnut (cremini) mushrooms, roughly chopped

300g (10½oz) oyster mushrooms, roughly torn

3 tbsp olive oil

5 garlic cloves, minced

1 tbsp dried mixed herbs

400g (14oz) can black beans, drained and rinsed

Crispy Gnocchi *with* Romesco Hummus

Serves 2

I'm always looking for comfort food options that feel grown-up and this is a current favourite. Perfect for snacking on while sitting on the sofa after a long day, sharing with friends over drinks, or just using the gnocchi as my dipping vessel for a fancy "chip and dip" evening.

Preheat your oven to 210°C (190°C fan/410°F/Gas 6–7) and line a baking sheet with baking parchment. Alternatively, preheat your air fryer to 190°C (375°F) and spray or drizzle the basket with vegetable oil.

Combine the breadcrumbs, dried mixed herbs, oil and some salt and pepper in a large mixing bowl and set aside.

Add the gnocchi to a pan of boiling water, cook for 2 minutes, then drain immediately.

Add the gnocchi to the breadcrumb mixture and gently toss to coat, then tip them onto the lined baking sheet or into the air fryer basket. Bake for 15–20 mins, tossing occasionally, until golden and crispy.

To make the romesco hummus, simply add all the ingredients to a food processor or blender along with 2 ice cubes and blitz until very smooth. Taste and add more salt if needed.

Spread the dip over a sharing plate, scatter over the quartered tomatoes then top with the crispy gnocchi. Sprinkle with some parsley and serve immediately.

35g (¾ cup) panko breadcrumbs

1 tbsp dried mixed herbs

1 tbsp vegetable oil, plus extra for spraying/drizzling

500g (1lb 2oz) gnocchi

100g (3½oz) cherry tomatoes, quartered

small handful of parsley, roughly chopped, to serve

salt and freshly ground black pepper

FOR THE ROMESCO HUMMUS

200g (7oz) chickpeas, drained and rinsed

100g (3½oz) roasted red (bell) peppers (the kind from a jar)

90g (3oz) sun dried tomatoes

juice of ½ lemon

1 garlic clove

1½ tbsp extra virgin olive oil

2 tbsp tahini (sesame paste)

1 tsp smoked paprika

½ tsp ground cumin

½ tsp salt

NOTE

To make this *even* speedier and easier, you can skip the dip and serve the crispy gnocchi with your favourite store-bought red (bell) pepper or smoky hummus.

Prep	Cook	Difficulty level	Protein per tart
10 mins	20–22 mins	3/5	9.7g (⅜oz)

Cannellini, Cheese + Chive Tarts

Serves 4

I love an accidental vegan discovery, and store-bought puff pastry has got to be one of the best. It really adds to the magic of this sort of meal, which is so satisfying in its flavour and simplicity. Using white beans to add a creamy element to recipes is one of my favourite nutritious hacks for adding an extra fibre and protein hit.

Preheat the oven to 210°C (190°C fan/410°F/Gas 6–7) and line a baking sheet with baking parchment.

Add a drizzle of olive oil to a pan set over a medium heat. Sauté the leek and garlic, along with a generous seasoning of salt and pepper, for 5–7 minutes until softened.

Add the cannellini beans, cheese, dried mixed herbs and lemon zest and juice to the pan and stir well. Use a potato masher to crush and break down the beans until they have a hummus-like consistency. Mix well, taste for seasoning, adding more salt and pepper if needed, then remove from the heat.

Place the pastry sheet on a chopping board and cut it into quarters, so you have 4 even rectangles, then transfer these to the lined baking sheet. Evenly spread the bean and leek mixture onto each pastry rectangle, leaving a 2cm (¾in) border around the edges. Fold the border over itself, onto the bean and leek mixture, to form a crust. Arrange some courgette slices on top of each tart, then generously drizzle the tarts with olive oil (especially the crusts) and season with salt and pepper.

Bake for 20–22 minutes until evenly golden. Scatter over the chives, then serve up the individual tarts with a peppery green salad.

olive oil, for frying/drizzling

1 leek, thinly sliced

2 garlic cloves, minced

400g (14oz) can cannellini beans, drained and rinsed

50g (1¾oz) meltable vegan Cheddar, grated

1 tsp dried mixed herbs

zest and juice of ½ lemon

320g (11oz) store-bought ready-rolled puff pastry (ensure vegan)

½ courgette (zucchini), thinly sliced

small handful of chives, finely chopped

peppery mixed salad, to serve

salt and freshly ground black pepper

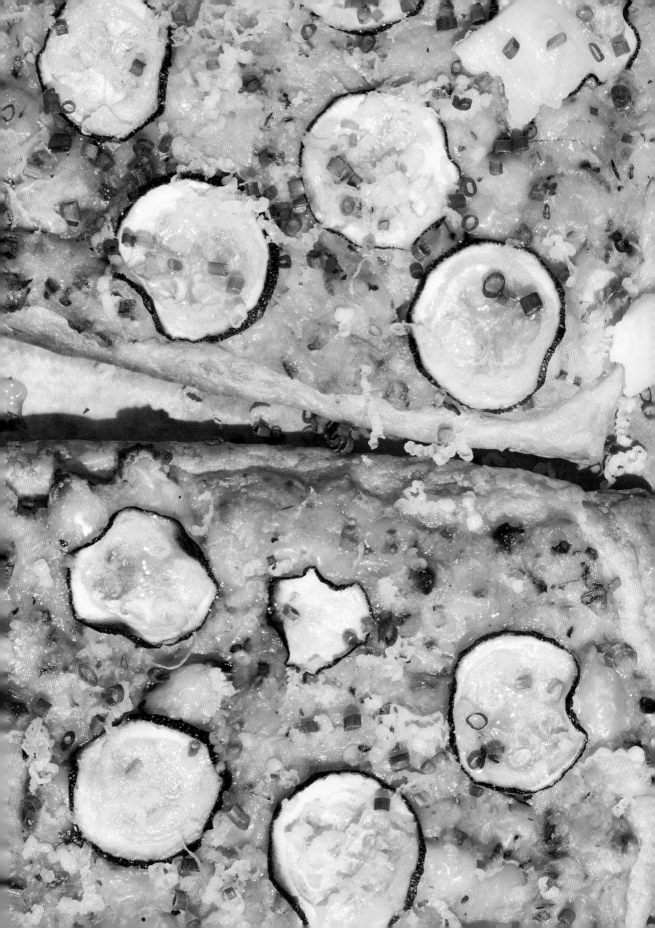

Prep	Cook	Difficulty level	Protein per serving
5 mins	30 mins	2/5	17.9g (⅝oz)

Gochujang + Black Bean Loaded Sweet Potatoes

Serves 3

I always have gochujang in my fridge – this spicy Korean pepper paste has an incredible subtle sweetness, thanks to its fermentation, and it is so versatile. It's a match made in speedy dinner heaven when paired with sweet potatoes, perfect for when you're short on time but don't want to compromise on nutrition.

Place the sweet potatoes in the microwave and cook at 800–1000W for 15 minutes, turning them over after 10 minutes. Use a sharp knife to check they are soft through, then place to one side to cool slightly.

Meanwhile, add the black beans to a large mixing bowl along with the coriander, garlic, ginger, spring onions, cheese, gochujang paste, paprika and cumin. Season well with salt and pepper then mix and roughly mash to combine everything.

Preheat your oven to 220°C (200°C fan/425°F/Gas 7) and line a baking sheet with baking parchment. Alternatively, preheat your air fryer to 200°C (400°F) and spray or drizzle the basket with vegetable oil.

When cool enough to handle, cut the sweet potatoes in half and scoop the flesh into the bowl with the black beans, keeping the skin intact. Mash and mix the sweet potato flesh into the beans, then load each potato skin with the mixture until you've used it all up. Place the loaded potato skins on the lined baking sheet or in the greased air fryer basket and spray or drizzle with a little oil. Cook in the oven or air fryer for 10–15 minutes, until the tops are golden.

Combine all the ingredients for the sesame sauce in a bowl and whisk until smooth (you may need to add a little more hot water to reach a drizzling consistency). Taste and add salt if needed. Serve the loaded sweet potatoes drizzled with the sesame sauce with a green salad on the side.

3 medium sweet potatoes (yams)

400g (14oz) can black beans, drained and rinsed

small handful of coriander (cilantro), finely chopped

3 garlic cloves, minced

thumb-sized piece of fresh root ginger, minced

3 spring onions (scallions), finely chopped

100g (3½oz) meltable vegan Cheddar, grated

1½ tbsp gochujang paste

1 tbsp smoked paprika

1 tsp ground cumin

olive oil, for drizzling/spraying

green salad, to serve

salt and freshly ground black pepper

FOR THE SESAME SAUCE

100g (½ cup minus 1 tbsp) tahini (sesame paste)

1 tbsp maple syrup

juice of 1 lime

60ml (4 tbsp) hot water

NOTE

If you're not a coriander lover, use chives instead!

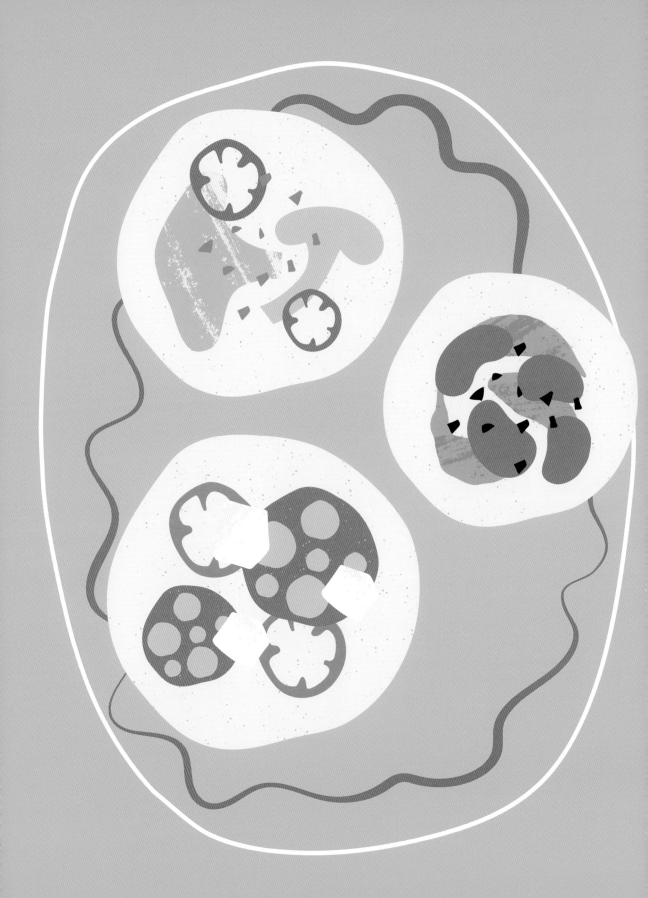

4

Prepped Plates

Three core recipes equals ten incredible suppers that will keep you feeling full and nourished with almost zero effort.

Tofu Chorizo

95

Smoky Tofu Chorizo Tacos

96

Three-bean Chorizo Chilli

100

Smoky Chorizo Burger

102

Mega Protein Meatballs

104

Manchurian Meatball Noodles

106

Spaghetti Meatballs

108

Peppercorn Meatballs + Mash

110

Seitan Chicken

113

Spinach, Ricotta + Chicken Quesadillas

114

Tuscan Chicken Pie

116

Lime + Lemongrass Noodle Bowl

118

Thai Green Chicken Curry

120

Prepped Plates

Prepped Plates

94

Tofu Chorizo

Makes about 750g (26oz)
(enough for the following 3 recipes)

If I could only make one meat replacement for the rest of my days, it would be this delicious smoky tofu chorizo. I've been making this recipe for years – it's so versatile, has a great texture and those beautiful umami flavours from the sun dried tomatoes add the best kick of flavour to any dish. Make up a batch on Sunday and use it throughout the week to make the recipes on pages 96, 100 and 102. Easy weeknight meals sorted.

Preheat your oven to 210°C (190°C fan/410°F/Gas 6–7) and line a baking tray (sheet) with baking parchment.

Using your hands, crumble the tofu into a bowl in very small pieces so it resembles the texture of minced (ground) meat (you can also use a food processor if the tofu is very firm). Add the spices, maple syrup, tomato purée, salt and pepper and mix thoroughly, then add the oil from the sun dried tomato jar and mix again.

Tip the mixture onto the lined baking tray, ensuring it's spread out evenly. Bake for 25 minutes, tossing the mixture every 3 minutes as it colours very quickly (add an extra drizzle of oil if it starts to dry out). Add the sun dried tomatoes to the baking tray and stir, then return to the oven for a further 5–10 minutes until the tofu is a deep brown colour with a slight char at the edges.

Remove from the oven and leave to cool, then transfer to a sealed container. This will keep in the fridge for 4–5 days or in the freezer for up to 1 month.

675g (1½lb) smoked extra-firm tofu, drained

6 tbsp smoked sweet paprika

2 tsp ground cayenne pepper (or to taste)

3 tsp ground cumin

6 tbsp maple syrup

9 tbsp tomato purée (paste)

3 tsp salt

3 tsp freshly ground black pepper

18 sun dried tomatoes, finely chopped, plus 12 tbsp oil from the jar (or use olive oil)

NOTE

Depending on the size of jar you're able to purchase, you may need to buy two jars of sun dried tomatoes to reach the stated quantity. If you don't have enough oil from the jar, simply top up with olive oil.

Smoky Tofu Chorizo Tacos

Serves 2–4 *(depending on hunger levels!)*

This is such a crowd-pleaser and is the perfect party food. Trust me, everyone around the table will devour these smoky and sticky tofu loaded tacos, meat-eaters and vegans alike.

250g (9oz) tofu chorizo (page 95)

8 mini corn or flour tortillas

150ml (⅔ cup) vegan sour cream

1 large avocado, halved and pitted

100g (3½oz) vegan feta

about 8 sliced jalapeños from a jar

small handful of coriander (cilantro), leaves picked and roughly chopped

lime wedges, for squeezing

Set a frying pan (skillet) over a low–medium heat and add the tofu chorizo. Toss and cook for 5 minutes until the tofu is hot, then transfer to a bowl and set aside. Place the pan back on the heat.

In batches, warm the tortillas in the hot pan, cooking for about 30 seconds on each side. Once hot, wrap them in a tea towel or cloth while you continue cooking the rest, to keep them warm and soft.

Add a dollop of sour cream to each warm tortilla, thinly slice the avocado flesh and add a couple of slices to each taco, then top with some of the warm tofu chorizo. Crumble over a little feta, add some jalapeños and coriander, then serve with lime wedges on the side for squeezing.

Three-bean Chorizo Chilli

Serves 4

I must admit, it takes a lot to get me excited about a chilli, but there's something about this one that means I make it on repeat. That it's a one-pot wonder always helps, but the smokiness of the chorizo really sets this apart from your usual weeknight favourite.

Add a glug of vegetable oil to a frying pan (skillet) set over a medium heat. Add the red onion, red pepper, chilli and garlic and sauté for 5–7 minutes until beginning to soften. Season well with salt and pepper then add the paprika, ground cumin and coriander and fry for a few seconds before deglazing the pan with the vinegar.

Add the stock, dark chocolate and sugar, then tip in the tomatoes, crushing them with your hands or a spoon as you add them. Stir everything well then add the mixed beans, cover the pan and reduce the heat to low. Simmer for 10 minutes, then add the chorizo to the chilli and remove the pan from the heat.

Cook the rice according to the packet instructions then serve it in bowls topped with the chilli. Dollop a spoonful of yogurt onto each then sprinkle with red onion and coriander and serve with lime wedges on the side for squeezing.

vegetable oil, for frying

1 red onion, finely chopped

1 red (bell) pepper, finely sliced

1 red chilli, finely chopped

3 garlic cloves, minced

1½ tsp smoked paprika

1 tsp ground cumin

1 tsp ground coriander

1 tbsp red wine vinegar

400ml (1¾ cups) hot vegan beef stock or vegetable stock

15g (½oz) dark chocolate (ensure vegan)

1 tsp soft light brown sugar

400g (14oz) can whole plum tomatoes

400g (14oz) can mixed beans, drained and rinsed

250g (9oz) tofu chorizo (page 95)

salt and freshly ground black pepper

TO SERVE

300g (10½oz) basmati rice

4 tbsp soy yogurt

1 red onion, finely sliced

small handful of coriander (cilantro), roughly chopped

lime wedges, for squeezing

Prep	Cook	Difficulty level	Protein per burger
10 mins	10 mins	3/5	19.6g (11/16oz)
(+ chilling)			

Smoky Chorizo Burger

Serves 4

This might just be my favourite burger in the whole book. Whether you want the full take-out experience or just an easy meat replacement, the patties are simple to prepare in advance and freeze really well.

Place all the ingredients for the patties (apart from the flour) into a large bowl and mix until completely combined (your hands are useful here). Add the flour, a little at a time, until the mixture just comes together. Season well with salt and pepper.

Divide the mixture into four equal patties then transfer to a plate and refrigerate for 30 minutes to firm up.

Meanwhile, combine all the ingredients for the black pepper aioli in a small bowl and set aside.

Add a drizzle of vegetable oil to a lidded frying pan (skillet) set over a medium heat. Fry the patties for 3 minutes on each side, then top each patty with a slice of cheese, place the lid on the pan and cook for 1 minute more to melt the cheese.

Now it's time to assemble. Spread a spoonful of aioli onto the brioche bun bottoms, then add some rocket and tomato slices, followed by a chorizo patty. Dollop on any remaining aioli, add some pickled red onions then drizzle with chilli oil. Add the bun tops and dive in.

vegetable oil, for frying

4 slices vegan smoked cheese

4 vegan brioche burger buns (or your favourite roll), split and toasted

handful of rocket (arugula)

1 beef tomato, sliced

50g (1¾oz) store-bought pickled red onions

chilli oil, for drizzling

salt and freshly ground black pepper

FOR THE PATTIES

150g (5½oz) tofu chorizo (page 95)

250g (9oz) vegan mince (vegan ground meat)

½ small red onion, finely chopped

5 sun dried tomatoes, finely chopped

1 tbsp smoked paprika

½ tbsp liquid smoke (optional)

1 tsp dried chilli (red pepper) flakes

½ tsp garlic powder

1–3 tbsp plain (all-purpose) flour

FOR THE BLACK PEPPER AIOLI

4 tbsp vegan mayo

1 garlic clove, minced

1 tsp cracked black pepper

NOTE

When making the patties, try to use a vegan mince that is "meaty" rather than dry or crumbly. I use Richmond Meat-Free Mince.

Prep	Cook	Difficulty level	Protein per serving
20 mins	0 mins	2/5	(5 meatballs)
			22.5g (¹³⁄₁₆oz)

Mega Protein Meatballs

Makes 30 meatballs / 6 servings
(enough for the following 3 recipes)

125g (4½oz) TVP mince (page 14)

250ml (1 cup) boiling water

100g (1¼ cups) fine golden breadcrumbs

5 tbsp dairy-free milk

325g (11½oz) medium-firm tofu, drained

small handful parsley, chopped

zest of ½ lemon

2 garlic cloves, minced

1 tbsp olive oil

1½ tsp Marmite (or other yeast extract)

1 tbsp plain (all-purpose) flour, plus extra if needed

1 tbsp dried mixed herbs

1 tbsp smoked paprika

½ tsp onion powder

salt and freshly ground black pepper

Textured vegetable protein (TVP) may not sound delicious, but it's one of my favourite affordable store cupboard ingredients. It's essentially a protein-packed flavour sponge that takes on the role of a ground beef substitute. These meatballs are so quick to make you can even whip them up on a weeknight! Make a batch and use them for the speedy weeknight suppers on pages 106, 108 and 110.

Place the TVP in a heatproof bowl and pour over the boiling water. Set aside for 10 minutes to allow it to absorb all the water.

Combine the breadcrumbs and milk in a small bowl and set this aside too.

Finely crumble the tofu into a large bowl then add all the remaining ingredients. When the TVP has rehydrated, squeeze out as much excess liquid as possible before adding it to the mixing bowl. Mix everything well, then add the soaked breadcrumbs to the bowl too, season generously with salt and pepper and mix again.

If the mixture doesn't bind together when pressed between your hands, add more flour, a little at a time, until it just holds together.

Form the mixture into 30 balls (each about 30g/1oz), compressing them tightly. Store them in a sealed container in the fridge for up to 5 days or the freezer for up to 1 month.

Prep	Cook	Difficulty level	Protein per serving
5 mins	15 mins	1/5	32.2g (1oz)

Manchurian Meatball Noodles

Serves 2

When I travelled across Southeast Asia, gobi Manchurian was the dish I ordered on repeat. I couldn't believe it wasn't more popular in the UK, so I had to make my own version to cure those cravings! The sauce is an Indo-Chinese fusion of sweet tangy flavours and it's perfect combined with my mega protein meatballs.

Add a glug of vegetable oil to a frying pan (skillet) set over a medium heat then fry the meatballs for 6–7 minutes until lightly coloured. Transfer to a plate and place the pan back on the heat.

Add the green pepper, spring onions, chilli, garlic and ginger to the pan, adding a little more oil if needed, and fry for 2–3 minutes until softened. Add the remaining sauce ingredients to the pan and mix well, then simmer for 2 minutes until it is well combined and hot through. Add the meatballs back to the pan and gently stir to coat them in the sauce.

Place the noodles in a heatproof bowl and pour over hot water from the kettle to warm them.

Drain the noodles, split them between two bowls, then spoon the meatballs and sauce over the top.

vegetable oil, for frying

10 mega protein meatballs (page 104)

300g (10½oz) precooked fresh udon noodles

FOR THE SAUCE

1 green (bell) pepper, thinly sliced

4 spring onions (scallions), chopped

1 red or green chilli, finely chopped

3 garlic cloves, minced

2.5cm (1in) piece of fresh root ginger, minced

6 tbsp ketchup

4 tbsp light soy sauce

2 tbsp sriracha or chilli sauce

2 tbsp rice wine vinegar

2 tsp caster (superfine) sugar

1 tsp freshly ground black pepper

Spaghetti Meatballs *with* Rocket + Mint Pesto

Serves 2

I'm pretty sure we all have a sad, half-emtpy bag of wilted rocket sitting in the bottom drawer of our fridge, so give it a new lease of life by whizzing it up into this pesto for a quick midweek meal. This method works with most salad leaves, but rocket adds extra pepperiness to this easy sauce.

To make the pesto, add all the ingredients to a blender or food processor, season generously with salt and pepper, then blitz until smooth. Add a little more olive oil if needed to blend it easily. Set aside.

Add a drizzle of vegetable oil to a frying pan (skillet) set over a medium–high heat. Fry the meatballs for 8 minutes until lightly coloured then add the asparagus and cook for a further 3 minutes until it turns bright green. Season well with salt and pepper and take the pan off the heat.

Meanwhile, in a large saucepan of salted boiling water, cook the spaghetti according to the packet instructions. Drain, reserving a mugful of pasta cooking water, then add the pasta back to the saucepan and toss with a drizzle of olive oil.

Add the pesto to the spaghetti and toss to completely coat the pasta, adding the reserved pasta cooking water a little at a time to loosen the pesto.

Add the asparagus, meatballs and cherry tomatoes to the pan and gently stir to warm everything through, then serve up in bowls.

olive oil, for frying/drizzling

10 mega protein meatballs (page 104)

250g (9oz) asparagus, roughly chopped and tough stems discarded

180g (6½oz) spaghetti (ensure vegan)

handful of mixed cherry tomatoes, halved

salt and freshly ground black pepper

FOR THE ROCKET + MINT PESTO

30g (1oz) rocket (arugula)

8–10 mint sprigs, leaves picked

45g (1½oz) cashew nuts

zest and juice of ½ lemon

1 garlic clove

2 tbsp nutritional yeast

4 tbsp olive oil, plus extra if needed

Peppercorn Meatballs + Mash

Serves 2

There's nothing I love more than finding an elevated version of my favourite comfort food – in this case, the humble sausage and mash. I've given it a Scandi twist with peas and lingonberry jam but it is great served with any greens.

To make the mash, place the potatoes into a large saucepan of cold, salted water and bring to the boil. Boil for about 15 minutes, or until you can easily pierce the potato with a fork, then drain and return to the pan. Add the remaining ingredients then mash until smooth.

Meanwhile, add a drizzle of vegetable oil to a frying pan (skillet) set over a medium–high heat. Fry the meatballs for 8–10 minutes until lightly coloured then transfer them to a plate.

To make the peppercorn sauce, place the pan back on the heat and add the crushed black peppercorns. Toast for 1 minute until fragrant, then add the butter, shallot and garlic and fry for 5 minutes until translucent. Add the vinegar to deglaze the pan, scraping up any brown bits, and continue to cook until all the liquid has disappeared. Stir in the remaining sauce ingredients, along with a pinch of salt, then reduce the heat to low and simmer for 5 minutes.

Add the meatballs back into the pan with the peppercorn sauce to heat through and get coated in the sauce.

Divide the mash between two plates and top with the meatballs and peppercorn sauce, then serve with peas and a dollop of cranberry or lingonberry jam.

vegetable oil, for frying

10 mega protein meatballs (page 104)

150g (5½oz) cooked peas, to serve

2 tbsp cranberry or lingonberry jam, to serve

salt and freshly ground black pepper

FOR THE PEPPERCORN SAUCE

2 tsp black peppercorns, roughly crushed using a pestle and mortar

1 tbsp vegan butter

1 shallot, finely diced

3 garlic cloves, minced

1 tbsp white wine vinegar

250ml (1 cup) vegan double (heavy) cream

1 tbsp vegan Worcestershire sauce

1 bay leaf

2 tbsp nutritional yeast

FOR THE MASH

2 medium potatoes (about 500g/1lb 2oz), peeled and cubed

4 tbsp dairy-free milk

1½ tbsp vegan butter

1 tbsp wholegrain mustard

Prep	Cook	Difficulty level	Protein per 50g (2oz)
30 mins	1 hour 30 mins (+ cooling)	5/5	9.9g (⅜oz)

Seitan Chicken

Makes about 1.3kg (3lb)
(enough for the following 4 recipes)

Could this be a vegan cookbook without a seitan recipe? Seitan is made from vital wheat gluten, a highly glutinous and protein-rich flour that, after being kneaded, takes on a "meaty" texture. When mixed with a few other flavours and simmered you get impressive chicken-like strands.

Add the silken tofu, cannellini beans and their liquid, vegetable oil, miso paste, lemon juice and garlic to a food processor and blend for 1 minute until smooth and silky. Add the vital wheat gluten, white pepper and salt to the processor and blend again for 30 seconds until combined and a stretchy, tacky dough has formed.

Turn the dough out onto a surface, knead for 10 minutes, then divide into 6 equal pieces. Roll each piece into a thin log about 30cm (12in) long. With each, knot the length of dough in the middle and tuck the ends into the middle knot. You should now have six individual knotted balls of dough. Tightly wrap each dough ball in a piece of muslin (cheesecloth) – or use baking parchment and string – ensuring each one is very tightly wrapped.

To make the brine, add the stock, garlic, onion and bay leaves to a large, deep, lidded pan and bring to a boil. Add the dough ball parcels and gently simmer for 1½ hours with the lid on.

Using a slotted spoon, remove the parcels from the brine and place them in a large bowl. Allow to cool for 20–30 minutes in their wrapping. Strain the remaining brine into a jug and stir in the vinegar and salt.

Once cool enough to handle, unwrap the seitan and tear it into large chunks. Place it in a large bowl or sealable container and pour over the brine. Cover and allow to cool at room temperature before placing in the fridge overnight (it will keep in here for up to 5 days). Your seitan is now ready to use. Shred further with a fork or use in chunks.

300g (10½oz) silken tofu, drained
400g (14oz) can cannellini beans, including the liquid from the can
4 tbsp vegetable oil
1 tbsp white miso paste
juice of ½ lemon
1 garlic clove, minced
320g (2¼ cups) vital wheat gluten (page 14)
½ tsp ground white pepper
½ tsp salt

FOR THE BRINE

2 litres (about 2 quarts) vegetable stock
3 garlic cloves, bruised
1 onion, halved
2 bay leaves
2 tbsp white vinegar
1 tsp salt

NOTE
This also freezes well. Simply place the cooked seitan chicken in a sealed container *without* the brine and store it in the freezer for up to 1 month.

Prep	Cook	Difficulty level	Protein per serving
10 mins	11 mins	2/5	28.1g (1oz)

Spinach, Ricotta + Chicken Quesadillas

Serves 4

If you're not quite converted to tofu yet (just give me time!), try this "ricotta" version layered between tortilla wraps for a speedy lunch.

Set a frying pan (skillet) over a medium heat and drizzle in the oil. Add the seitan chicken and fry for about 5 minutes until golden brown. Add the spinach and garlic and cook for 2 minutes to wilt the spinach. Transfer the mixture to a bowl and leave to cool.

Place all the tofu ricotta ingredients, along with a pinch each of salt and pepper, in a blender or food processor and blitz until it forms a smooth paste, like the consistency of a thick hummus (if it's too thick, add an extra splash of milk). Scrape this into the bowl with the seitan and spinach, add the grated cheese and mix everything together. Season to taste with salt and pepper.

Divide the mixture evenly between each tortilla wrap, spreading it to cover half of each wrap, then fold each wrap in half, to enclose the filling.

Wipe out the frying pan and set it back over a medium heat. In batches, fry the quesadillas for 2 minutes, then flip and cover while they cook for another 2 minutes until both sides are golden brown and the cheese is melty.

Slice in half and serve with a mixed salad.

1 tbsp vegetable oil

250g (9oz) seitan chicken (page 113), shredded

250g (9oz) baby spinach

3 garlic cloves, minced

80g (3oz) meltable vegan Cheddar, grated

4 tortilla wraps

mixed salad leaves, to serve

salt and freshly ground black pepper

FOR THE TOFU RICOTTA

250g (9oz) medium-firm tofu, drained

2 tbsp nutritional yeast

2 tbsp hummus

juice of ½ lemon

1 tsp Dijon mustard

½ tsp onion powder

1 tbsp dairy-free milk

Prep	Cook	Difficulty level	Protein per serving
5 mins	30 mins	2/5	36g (1¼oz)

Tuscan Chicken Pie

Serves 3

This pie is perfect for midweek cold nights when you need something wholesome, nourishing, warm and comforting. A super-rewarding one-pot dinner.

Place an ovenproof frying pan (skillet) or shallow casserole dish (about 25cm/10in) over a medium heat and drizzle in 1 tablespoon of the oil. Add the shallots and garlic and sweat down for 5 minutes until translucent.

Add the seitan chicken and fry for 6–8 minutes until it starts to brown, then add the spinach, sun dried tomatoes, nutritional yeast, dried mixed herbs and paprika and cook until the spinach has wilted, stirring to encourage it. Pour in the white beans and their liquid, and the cream, then season to taste with salt and pepper.

Cover the pan with the puff pastry sheet and trim off any excess, then make a hole in the middle of the pastry using a knife to allow the steam to escape. Mix the remaining 1 tablespoon of oil with the maple syrup then brush this over the pastry.

Slide the pie into the oven and bake for about 15 minutes, or until the pie top is golden and flaky. Allow to stand for a couple of minutes before serving with your favourite veggies.

2 tbsp vegetable oil

2 shallots, finely chopped

3 garlic cloves, minced

250g (9oz) seitan chicken (page 113), shredded

200g (7oz) baby spinach

6 sun dried tomatoes, chopped

1 tbsp nutritional yeast

1 tbsp dried mixed herbs

1 tsp smoked paprika

400g (14oz) can white beans, including the liquid from the can

250ml (1 cup) dairy-free double (heavy) cream

1 sheet store-bought ready-rolled puff pastry (ensure vegan)

1 tbsp maple syrup

salt and freshly ground black pepper

117

Lime + Lemongrass Noodle Bowl

Serves 2

In my opinion, lemongrass is a criminally underused ingredient. You can buy sticks of lemongrass and keep them in the freezer or simply use lemongrass paste for ease (you can usually find it in the spice aisle of supermarkets). These noodles are so light and fresh but packed with flavour – this is a regular midweek winner for me.

Add 1 tablespoon of the vegetable oil to a large frying pan (skillet) set over a medium heat. Add the seitan chicken chunks to the hot pan and fry for about 6–8 minutes until lightly golden all over.

Reduce the heat slightly, then add the remaining 1 tablespoon of oil followed by the pepper, sugar snap peas, lemongrass, garlic and ginger. Stir fry for 2–3 minutes, until the peppers are starting to soften, then add the lime juice, soy sauce, sesame oil, sugar and 4 tablespoons of the seitan brine and mix well.

Place the noodles in a heatproof bowl and pour over hot water from the kettle to warm them. Drain the noodles and add them to the pan along with the Thai basil leaves, stirring gently to combine everything.

Serve in bowls sprinkled with chilli flakes (if using), some extra Thai basil leaves and lime wedges on the side for squeezing.

2 tbsp vegetable oil

180g (6½oz) seitan chicken (page 113), plus 4 tbsp brine (or use water)

1 yellow or red (bell) pepper, thinly sliced

200g (7oz) sugar snap peas, sliced lengthways

2 lemongrass stalks (or 1½ tbsp lemongrass paste), tough stems removed and finely chopped

3 garlic cloves, minced

4cm (1½in) piece of fresh root ginger, minced

juice of 1½ limes, plus extra wedges to serve

2 tbsp light soy sauce

1 tbsp toasted sesame oil

1 tbsp soft light brown sugar

150g (5½oz) precooked fresh flat rice noodles

handful of Thai basil, leaves picked and cut into ribbons, plus extra to serve

pinch of dried chilli (red pepper) flakes (optional)

119

Prep	Cook	Difficulty level	Protein per serving
15 mins	30 mins	4/5	22g (13⁄16oz) (without optional extras)

Protein per serving: 22g ($^{13}\!/_{16}$oz) (without optional extras)

Thai Green Chicken Curry

Serves 4

Making your own curry paste may seem like an extravagance but, trust me, this fragrant and light recipe is so worth the effort. It absolutely bursts with flavour!

Add all the curry paste ingredients to a food processor or mini chopper and blend to a smooth paste.

Add the seitan chicken and 2 heaped tablespoons of the curry paste to a bowl. Mix well to coat.

Place a large saucepan over a medium heat and drizzle in the oil. Fry the coated seitan for 6–8 minutes until golden, then remove it from the pan and set aside.

Set the pan back over the heat then add the remaining curry paste and fry for 3–4 minutes until fragrant. Add the coconut milk and vegetable stock and bring to a simmer. Add the potatoes to the pan and simmer them in the fragrant milk for 8–10 minutes, or until tender.

Place the cooked seitan back in the pan, along with the mangetout and cook for 3–4 minutes, then stir in the cashews.

This is lovely served just as it is, but I like to take it to the next level with some optional extras. Toss the beansprouts, red chilli, mint and coriander together. Serve the curry over cooked rice then top it with the tossed salad.

300g (10½oz) seitan chicken (page 113)

1 tbsp vegetable oil

400ml (14oz) can coconut milk

500ml (2 cups) hot vegetable stock

300g (10½oz) baby potatoes, halved or quartered

150g (5½oz) mangetout (snow peas)

80g (3oz) cashew nuts, toasted

FOR THE CURRY PASTE

30g (1oz) coriander (cilantro)

30g (1oz) Thai basil leaves

4 lime leaves, chopped

5cm (2in) piece of fresh root ginger, roughly chopped

2 banana shallots, chopped

4 garlic cloves, sliced

2 green chillies, deseeded and roughly chopped

2 lemongrass stalks (or 1½ tbsp lemongrass paste), tough stems removed and finely chopped

5 tbsp vegetable oil

2 tsp coriander seeds, toasted

1 tsp cumin seeds, toasted

2 tsp soft light brown sugar

1½ tsp salt

OPTIONAL EXTRAS

150g (5½oz) beansprouts

1 red chilli, finely sliced

small handful of mint leaves

small handful of coriander (cilantro) leaves

400g (14oz) cooked basmati rice

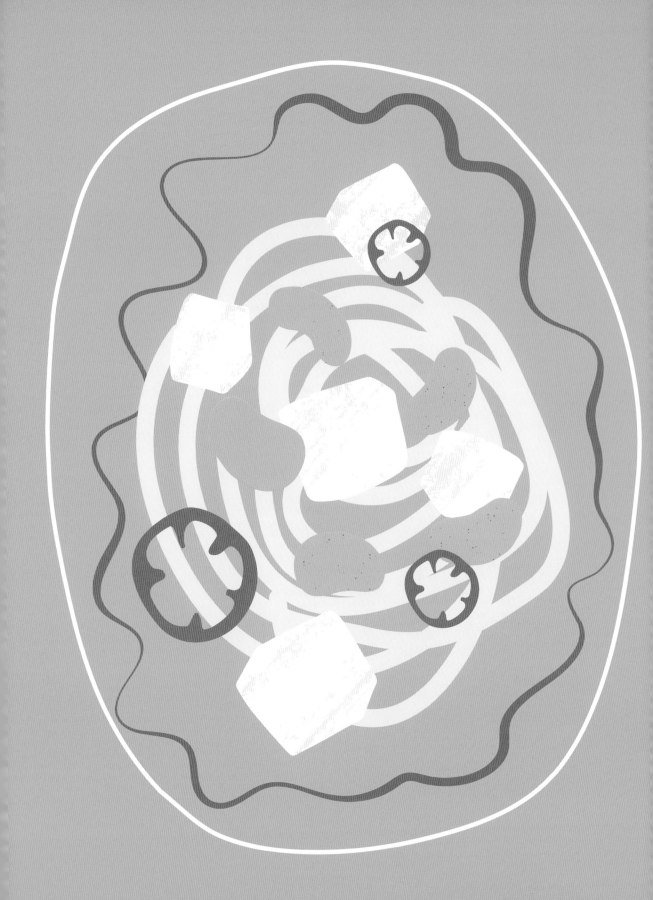

5

Protein-
Packed
Plates

Perfect post-exercise or when you need a boost, these easy high-protein recipes pack a punch, with at least 20% of the calories in each recipe dedicated to this essential nutrient.

The Reset Quinoa Bowl
126

Sticky Hasselback Tofu *with* Cashew Slaw
128

Herby Gyros *with* Tzatziki
131

Lahmacun-inspired Smashed Tacos
134

Peanut + Sesame Soba Salad
136

Best Ever Burrito
138

Chilli Jam Tahini Noodles
140

Green Skillet Lasagne
142

The Reset Quinoa Bowl *with* Tofu Feta

Serves 4

This recipe feels like a healthy relationship – it's always going to be there to pick you up once you've finished a heavy weekend. Prep this for work lunches on a Sunday and you'll feel super smug throughout the week.

Combine the quinoa and vegetable stock in a saucepan and set over a medium heat. Bring to a boil, then reduce to a simmer and cook, covered, for about 15 minutes. The stock should have been absorbed and the quinoa should be tender. Transfer to a large mixing bowl and set aside to cool.

To make the tofu feta, add the olive oil, lemon zest and juice, garlic, nutritional yeast, miso paste, oregano or mint and salt to another large bowl and whisk to form a dressing. Add the tofu and toss until it is completely coated.

Stir the onion, tomato, cucumber, chickpeas, basil and sumac with the cooled quinoa.

Add the tofu feta to the salad, being sure to scrape in all the dressing, then mix again so everything is well combined. Season with salt and pepper then serve sprinkled with a little extra sumac.

150g (scant 1 cup) quinoa, rinsed

350ml (1½ cups) hot vegetable stock

1 red onion, finely chopped

1 large salad tomato, cut into small chunks

½ cucumber, diced

400g (14oz) can chickpeas, drained and rinsed

handful of basil, leaves torn

1 tbsp sumac, plus extra to serve

FOR THE TOFU FETA

4 tbsp olive oil

zest and juice of ½ lemon

1 garlic clove, minced

2 tbsp nutritional yeast

1 tsp white miso paste

1 tsp dried oregano or mint

1 tsp salt

300g (10½oz) extra-firm tofu, drained and cut into 2cm (¾in) cubes

Sticky Hasselback Tofu *with* Cashew Slaw

Serves 2

If you haven't guessed by now, I'm a BIG advocate of tofu, and this is the perfect example of what I eat on a weekly basis. Glazed tofu with veggies equals lots of nutrition, minimal fuss and even less clean-up. It's the perfect dish to make me feel great post-workout.

Slice the block of tofu lengthways to form two equal "fillets". Now make diagonal consecutive cuts into the surface of each piece, only going about halfway through the tofu.

Mix together the soy sauce, sesame oil, mirin, maple syrup and ginger in a sealable container. Add the tofu to the marinade, ensuring it is fully covered, seal the lid and leave in the fridge to marinate for 30 minutes (or overnight). If you're short on time you can simply cook the tofu straight away.

Preheat your air fryer to 200°C (400°F) or your oven to 200°C (180°C fan/400°F/Gas 6). Line a small baking tray (that will fit into your air fryer) with foil or baking parchment.

Remove the tofu from the marinade (reserving the excess marinade) and place it on the prepared baking tray, cut-side up. Air fry the tofu for 20 minutes, or roast it in the oven for 30 minutes, basting with the reserved marinade every 5 minutes.

Combine all the slaw ingredients in a bowl and mix well. Divide the slaw between plates then top with the sticky hasselback tofu. Drizzle with any remaining marinade then sprinkle with sesame seeds before serving.

400g (14oz) block extra-firm tofu, drained

4 tbsp light soy sauce

2 tbsp sesame oil

2 tbsp mirin

1½ tbsp maple syrup

2.5cm (1in) piece of fresh root ginger, minced

toasted sesame seeds, to serve

FOR THE CASHEW SLAW

½ sweetheart cabbage, finely shredded

1 large carrot, julienned or cut into ribbons

½ red onion, finely sliced

50g (2oz) roasted and salted cashew nuts

juice of 1 lime

1 tbsp maple syrup

pinch of salt

Prep	Cook	Difficulty level	Protein per serving
25 mins	25 mins	3/5	21.4g (¾oz)

Herby Gyros *with* Tzatziki

Serves 4

Greece is one of my favourite places to visit – I love the people, the heat and (of course) the food! Just eating this takes me back to sitting by the beach, stuffing my face with double carbs, spiced vegan koftas and a fresh and garlicky tzatziki... absolute heaven.

Begin by cooking the fries according to the packet instructions, 2 minutes less than the packet timing states. Set aside.

Now make the quick pickled onions. Combine all the ingredients in a small bowl and scrunch them together a little with your hands. Set aside.

Next, make the tzatziki. Combine all ingredients in a small bowl and season to taste with salt and pepper. Set aside.

Preheat your grill (broiler) to medium–high and line a baking sheet with foil.

Combine all the ingredients for the koftas in a large bowl (apart from the oil), season well with salt and pepper, then mix thoroughly. The mix should hold together when squeezed – if it's a little dry, add a drizzle of oil and mix again. Form the kofta mixture into about 8 small log shapes and place them onto the prepared baking sheet.

Grill the koftas for 7–10 minutes, turning them regularly, until golden. During the final minute of cooking, add the cooked fries to the tray to heat through.

To assemble the gyros, top your toasted flatbreads with some sliced tomato and lettuce. Add a couple of koftas to each then load up with dollops of tzatziki, some quick pickled onions and a handful of fries. Wrap the flatbread around the filling and get stuck in.

200g (7oz) frozen oven fries

4 flatbreads, toasted

2 salad tomatoes, sliced

1 Little Gem lettuce, shredded

salt and freshly ground black pepper

FOR THE QUICK PICKLED ONIONS

½ red onion, finely sliced

juice of 1 lemon

½ tsp salt

FOR THE TZATZIKI

150g (generous 1 cup) dairy-free Greek yogurt

⅓ cucumber, deseeded and grated

small handful of mint leaves, finely chopped

1 garlic clove, minced

juice of ½ lemon

drizzle of olive oil

FOR THE KOFTAS

250g (9oz) vegan mince (vegan ground meat) (the "meaty" type)

handful of coriander (cilantro), finely chopped

handful of parsley, finely chopped

1 red chilli, deseeded and finely chopped

2 garlic cloves, minced

1 tbsp smoked paprika

1 tsp ground cumin

½ tsp ground coriander

½ tsp ground cinnamon

drizzle of olive oil (if needed)

Lahmacun-inspired Smashed Tacos

Serves 2–4 *(depending on hunger levels!)*

I adore Turkish and Middle Eastern food, so this recipe is on repeat in my kitchen thanks to the delicious flavour combinations. For a quick WFH lunch, double the mix and store it in the fridge – you can then simply smash it onto your tacos and fry them up whenever needed.

Place the TVP in a heatproof bowl and pour over the boiling water. Set aside for 10 minutes to allow it to absorb all the water.

Place the grated onion in a small bowl along with a generous pinch of salt. Scrunch it with your hands a little then leave it to one side.

Meanwhile, place the kidney beans in a large mixing bowl and squish them with your hands or a potato masher until semi-smooth. Add the garlic, parsley, tomato purée, oil and all the spices, then mix well.

Remove the TVP from the bowl, squeezing out as much liquid as possible, and transfer it to the bowl with the kidney beans. Squeeze the onion in the same way, to remove any excess liquid, then add this to the bowl too and mix well.

Evenly spread about 1 tablespoon of the mixture onto each mini tortilla.

Add a drizzle of vegetable oil to a non-stick frying pan (skillet) set over a medium–high heat. In batches, fry the tortillas "meat"-side down for 2–3 minutes until golden, then flip them to warm the other side for a few moments. Keep them warm in a low oven while you cook the rest.

Mix the tahini and garlic powder together in a small bowl, adding a splash of water to thin the mixture until it has a drizzle-able consistency.

Serve the tacos with a drizzle of the tahini sauce, the pomegranate seeds and some extra parsley.

200g (7oz) TVP mince (page 14)

500ml (2 cups) boiling water

1 small onion, coarsely grated

400g (14oz) can kidney beans, drained and rinsed

2 garlic cloves, minced

small handful of parsley, chopped, plus extra to serve

1 tbsp tomato purée (paste)

2 tbsp vegetable oil, plus extra for frying

1 tbsp smoked paprika

1 tsp ground cumin

1 tsp ground caraway seeds

½ tsp ground cayenne pepper

½ tsp allspice

½ tsp ground coriander

8 mini tortillas

handful of pomegranate seeds, to serve

salt and freshly ground black pepper

FOR THE TAHINI SAUCE

2 tbsp tahini (sesame paste)

½ tsp garlic powder

Prep	Cook	Difficulty level	Protein per serving
10 mins	10 mins (+ chilling)	2/5	32.6g (1oz)

Peanut + Sesame Soba Salad

Serves 4

I have such a soft spot for cold noodle salads; they feel like a far more luxurious version of a supermarket pasta salad. This particular version is perfect for meal prepping and will keep in the fridge for up to five days. Using soba noodles increases the protein content and you can always mix up the veggies to keep things exciting and seasonal.

Add the TVP to a bowl, pour over the hot stock, then leave to rehydrate for 10 minutes.

Meanwhile, in a frying pan (skillet) set over a medium heat, fry the spring onions, garlic and ginger in 1 tablespoon of the vegetable oil for about 2 minutes until softened. Transfer to a food processor or blender, along with all the other dressing ingredients, then blitz until smooth. Set aside.

Pop the pan back over a medium heat and add the remaining 2 tablespoons of vegetable oil. Remove the TVP from the bowl, squeezing out as much liquid as possible, then add it to the hot pan. Fry for 6–8 minutes, stirring regularly, until lightly browned. Set aside to allow it to cool a little.

Cook the soba noodles according to the packet instructions then drain and rinse them under cold water.

In a large bowl, combine the red cabbage, carrots, edamame, radishes, noodles, TVP and dressing, tossing well to ensure everything is well mixed. Taste and add a little salt and pepper if needed, then drizzle with chilli oil and sprinkle with sesame seeds and the reserved spring onion greens before serving.

100g (3½oz) TVP mince (page 14)

200ml (generous ¾ cup) hot vegetable stock

3 tbsp vegetable oil

200g (7oz) soba noodles

½ red cabbage, thinly shredded

2 carrots, peeled and julienned

150g (5½oz) edamame beans

handful of radishes, finely sliced

salt and freshly ground black pepper

FOR THE DRESSING

5 spring onions (scallions), roughly chopped (green ends reserved for garnish)

5 garlic cloves, minced

4cm (1½in) piece of fresh root ginger, minced

3 tbsp light soy sauce

2 tbsp tahini (sesame paste)

2 tbsp peanut butter

1½ tbsp rice wine vinegar

1½ tbsp soft light brown sugar

1 tbsp toasted sesame oil

juice of 2 limes

200ml (generous ¾ cup) water

TO SERVE

chilli oil

sesame seeds

Prep	Cook	Difficulty level	Protein per burrito
10 mins	20 mins	3/5	22g (13⁄16oz)

Best Ever Burrito

Serves 4

There are two types of people in this world: those who can perfectly wrap a burrito and those whose wrap totally falls apart, usually onto their shirt. This recipe is worth mastering!

Place the TVP in a heatproof bowl and add the soy sauce and stock cube. Pour over the boiling water, mix well to dissolve the stock cube and leave to one side to rehydrate for 10 minutes.

Set a frying pan (skillet) over a medium heat and drizzle in the oil. When hot, add the onion and garlic and sweat for 5 minutes. Season well with salt and pepper then push the onion and garlic to the side of the pan.

Remove the TVP from the bowl, squeezing out as much liquid as possible, then add it to the frying pan. Fry for 5–7 minutes until it starts to turn golden, then mix it with the onion and garlic.

Add the tomato purée, paprika, cumin and chilli powder and fry for 1 minute until fragrant. Next, stir in the black beans, sugar and coriander stalks and simmer for a few minutes to get everything nice and hot.

Meanwhile, microwave your rice according to the packet instructions. Once the rice is cooked, combine it with the lime juice and season with a little salt and pepper.

Spoon a quarter of the hot burrito filling into a log-shaped pile in the centre of a tortilla wrap. Top with a quarter of the Cheddar, a few jalapeños (if using), a quarter of the rice, a couple of slices of avocado and some coriander leaves. Fold up both ends of the wrap then tightly wrap it up to enclose the filling. Repeat with the other wraps and filling.

Wipe out the frying pan and place it back over a medium heat. In batches, fry the burritos seam-side down for 2 minutes, then flip and cook for another 2 minutes until crisp all over. Wrap the burritos in foil, slice them in half and serve with sour cream for dipping and dolloping.

75g (2¾oz) TVP mince (page 14)

1 tbsp light soy sauce

½ vegan beef stock cube

150ml (⅔ cup) boiling water

drizzle of olive oil

1 red onion, chopped

3 garlic cloves, minced

1½ tbsp tomato purée (paste)

2 tsp smoked paprika

1 tsp ground cumin

½ tsp chilli powder

400g (14oz) can black beans, drained and rinsed

1 tsp soft light brown sugar

handful of coriander (cilantro), stalks and leaves separated; stalks finely chopped

1 pouch (about 220g/8oz) spicy Mexican-style microwavable rice

juice of 1 lime

4 large tortilla wraps

60g (2¼oz) meltable vegan Cheddar

80g (3oz) pickled jalapeño slices (optional)

1 avocado, halved, pitted and sliced (optional)

4 tbsp vegan sour cream, to serve

salt and freshly ground black pepper

Chilli Jam Tahini Noodles

Serves 3

This chapter wouldn't be complete without some speedy noodles, and this fresh and moreish take is a weeknight staple in our house. They're so easy to pull together and, thanks to the curried tempeh crumble, have an addictive crunch!

Preheat your oven or air fryer to 220°C (200°C fan/425°F/Gas 7).

To make the curried tempeh crumble, break apart the tempeh into pieces about the size of your fingertip. Add this to a bowl along with the curry powder, soy sauce and agave syrup then season with salt and pepper and mix well. Tip the mixture onto a lined baking sheet or into your air fryer basket and drizzle with the olive oil. Bake for 15–18 minutes in the oven, or 12–15 minutes in the air fryer, stirring halfway through to ensure it cooks evenly, until golden. Set aside.

Meanwhile, prepare the quick pickled cucumber. Add the sugar, salt and vinegar to a large heatproof bowl then add the just-boiled water and stir to dissolve the sugar and salt. Slice the cucumber into thin matchsticks then add it to the bowl and mix well. Place in the fridge until ready to serve.

Add the tahini, chilli jam, soy sauce and lime juice to a small bowl. While whisking, add the cold water a little at a time until you have a smooth dressing (adding the water in this way prevents the tahini from seizing).

Bring a large pan of water to the boil then submerge the noodles for a few seconds to refresh them. Drain the noodles then add them back to the pan along with the tahini sauce and the spring onions. Stir over a low heat to combine then season with salt and pepper to taste.

Divide the noodles between plates, then top with the curried tempeh crumble, some coriander leaves, reserved spring onion greens and a sprinkle of sesame seeds. Serve with the quick pickled cucumber and lime wedges on the side for squeezing.

80g (3oz) tahini (sesame paste)

50g (1¾oz) chilli jam

2 tbsp light soy sauce

juice of 1 lime

100ml (3½fl oz) cold water

400g (14oz) precooked fresh wheat noodles (ensure vegan)

2 spring onions (scallions), finely chopped, green ends reserved for garnish

salt and freshly ground black pepper

FOR THE CURRIED TEMPEH CRUMBLE

260g (9oz) block of tempeh

1 tsp curry powder

1 tbsp light soy sauce

1 tbsp agave syrup

1 tbsp olive oil

FOR THE QUICK PICKLED CUCUMBER

1 tbsp caster (superfine) sugar

1 tsp salt

2½ tbsp rice wine vinegar

100ml (3½fl oz) just-boiled water

1 medium cucumber

TO SERVE

coriander (cilantro) leaves, roughly torn

sesame seeds

lime wedges, for squeezing

Green Skillet Lasagne

Makes 4

I don't like to play favourites, but this beauty encompasses
everything I love about pasta dishes. The vibrant herby sauce
marries up so well with the cream cheese topping. Swap out
the "chicken" for any preferred protein option.

Add 1 tablespoon of olive oil to a roughly 28cm (11in) ovenproof
frying pan (skillet) set over a medium heat. When hot, add the vegan
chicken chunks and fry for 6–8 minutes until lightly browned all over.
Sprinkle in the oregano and chilli flakes during the final minute
of cooking, then transfer the contents of the pan to a plate.

Place the pan back on the heat to make the green sauce. Add
1 tablespoon of olive oil, along with the shallots, courgette and garlic.
Sauté for 5 minutes until softening and lightly golden. Add the lemon
juice to deglaze, scraping up any flavour from the base of the pan.
Add the nutmeg and mustard seeds, followed by the vegetable stock,
spinach and basil. Stir to wilt the leaves, then transfer the mixture to
a blender and blitz until smooth. Scrape the green sauce back into the
pan, season with salt and pepper, then set over a low–medium heat.

Once the green sauce comes to a simmer, add the broken lasagne
sheets, stir to coat, then push them under the sauce. The sauce
should now completely cover the lasagne sheets – if not, add a little
water to the pan. Simmer for 10 minutes.

Preheat your grill (broiler) to medium.

Combine all the ingredients for the cream cheese topping, season
with salt and pepper then set aside.

Add the vegan chicken chunks back to the pan, along with the frozen
peas, and stir gently to combine. Dot the lasagne with the cream
cheese topping then scatter with the grated cheese. Place the lasagne
under the grill for 8–10 minutes until the top is golden and bubbling,
then allow to stand for 5 minutes before serving.

1 tbsp olive oil

320g (11½oz) vegan chicken chunks
(see page 113 for homemade)

1 tsp dried oregano

½ tsp dried chilli (red pepper) flakes

300g (10½oz) lasagne sheets
(ensure vegan), broken into rough
pieces

200g (7oz) frozen peas

40g (1½oz) meltable vegan
Cheddar, grated

salt and freshly ground black pepper

FOR THE GREEN SAUCE

1 tbsp olive oil

2 shallots, finely chopped

1 courgette (zucchini), chopped

3 garlic cloves, minced

juice of ½ lemon

½ tsp ground nutmeg

1 tsp mustard seeds

600ml (2½ cups) hot vegetable
stock

250g (9oz) baby spinach

handful of basil, leaves picked and
roughly chopped

FOR THE CREAM
CHEESE TOPPING

150g (5½oz) vegan cream cheese

small handful of tarragon, leaves
picked and chopped

zest of 1 lemon

1 tbsp olive oil

1 tbsp nutritional yeast

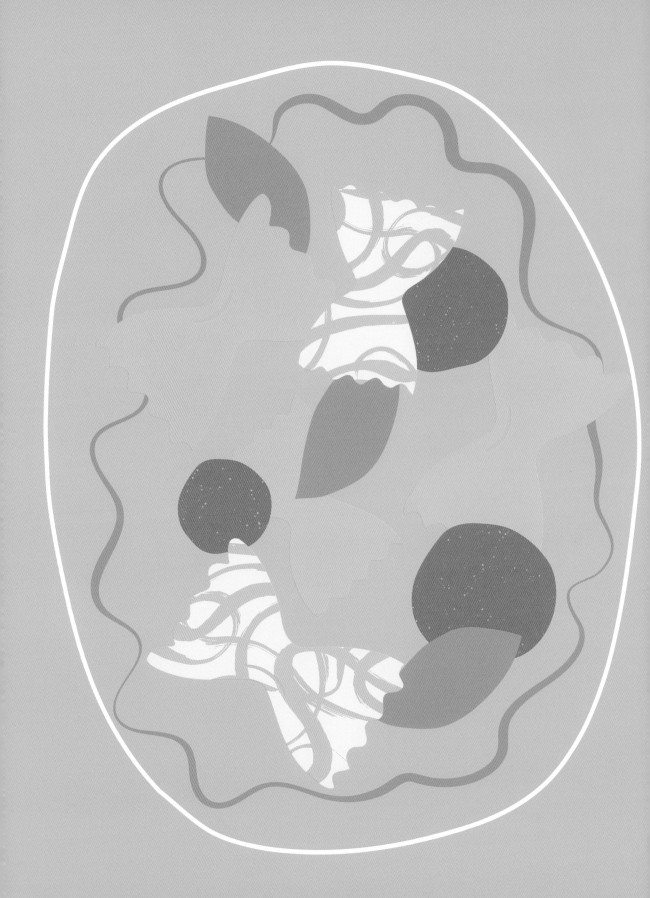

6

Comforting
Plates

Recipes that feel like a hug – perfect for eating in your pyjamas or sharing with your nearest and dearest.

Cheesy Ramen *with* Crispy Mushrooms
148
Leek + Sausage Orzotto
150
Charred Cauli Traybake *with* Cauli Leaf Pesto
153
Courgette *(kind of)* Carbonara
154
Hug-in-a-bowl Date Stew
156
Harissa Celeriac + Tofu Skewers *with* Jewelled Couscous
158
Tofu + Walnut Bolognese
160
Elly's Welly
162
Sticky Tofu Fillet *with* Red Wine Jus
164
Lasagne *with* White Bean Béchamel
167
Double Mushroom Brisket + Lentil Ragù
169
Butter Chickpea Curry
172
Creamy Coconut + Tofu Noodle Soup
174

Prep	Cook	Difficulty level	Protein per serving
5 mins	35 mins	4/5	28g (1oz)

Cheesy Ramen *with* Crispy Mushrooms

Serves 2

Finely sliced and roasted shiitake mushrooms go ultra-crisp and make for a great textural balance with this rich "cheesy" broth. So comforting; it feels rude not to eat it in your PJs.

Preheat your oven to 220°C (200°C fan/425°F/Gas 7) and line a baking sheet with baking parchment.

Slice the top off the garlic bulb and place it on a sheet of foil. Drizzle it with the vegetable oil and season with a pinch of salt then wrap the foil around it and bake for 25–30 minutes until soft. Once cool enough to handle, squeeze the soft flesh into a small bowl and mash it with a fork. Add the remaining paste ingredients to the bowl and mix together until fully combined. Set aside.

Meanwhile, add the shiitake mushrooms, vegetable oil, soy sauce, maple syrup and paprika to a medium bowl and mix until all the mushrooms are fully coated. Tip the mushrooms on the prepared baking sheet and place in the oven for 20–25 minutes, stirring halfway through, until golden and crispy (the garlic bulb and mushrooms can be in the oven at the same time).

Next, add a drizzle of oil to a frying pan (skillet) set over a medium–high heat. Fry the shredded cabbage for 3–5 minutes until it is charred in places but still retains some bite. Set aside.

Cook the ramen noodles according to the packet instructions then drain.

Now it's time to assemble. Into each serving bowl, add half of the paste then pour the hot stock, whisking to emulsify. Divide the noodles and cabbage evenly between the bowls, then sprinkle with some crispy mushrooms, cheese and chives.

vegetable oil, for frying

1 sweetheart cabbage, shredded

300g (10½oz) fresh ramen noodles (ensure vegan)

600ml (2½ cups) hot vegetable stock

60g (2¼oz) meltable vegan Cheddar, finely grated

handful of chives, finely chopped

red chilli, sliced, to serve (optional)

FOR THE PASTE

1 large garlic bulb

1 tbsp vegetable oil

pinch of salt

2 tbsp white miso paste

2 tbsp tahini (sesame paste)

1 tbsp sesame oil

1 tsp gochujang

3 tbsp nutritional yeast

FOR THE CRISPY MUSHROOMS

150g (5½oz) shiitake mushrooms, stems discarded and finely sliced

1 tbsp vegetable oil

1 tbsp light soy sauce

1 tbsp maple syrup

1 tsp smoked paprika

Leek + Sausage Orzotto

Serves 4

Leeks are my top comfort-food vegetable because they remind me of big bowls of sloppy risotto. I created this dish with the same vibe in mind but with far less faff, which is a big win as far as I'm concerned.

Add a drizzle of olive oil to a deep-sided frying pan (skillet) set over a medium heat and fry the sausage for 5–6 minutes until lightly browned. Add the mustard, agave syrup and a pinch of salt and mix well, then transfer the sausages to a plate and keep them warm. Place the pan back on the heat.

Add 2 tablespoons of the butter to the pan then add the leeks along with a generous pinch of salt. Cook the leeks for 10–15 minutes until softened.

Add the orzo, garlic and thyme to the leeks and fry for 2 minutes, then add the wine to deglaze the pan, scraping up any brown bits. Allow the liquid to completely disappear, then pour in the hot stock and season well with salt and pepper.

Bring to the boil and cook for 12 minutes, stirring regularly, until the orzo is almost cooked and most of the stock has been absorbed. Stir in the broccoli and white beans and cook for a further 6 minutes, or until the orzo and broccoli are tender.

Stir through the cream, nutritional yeast, lemon zest and juice and the remaining 1 tablespoon of butter. Taste for seasoning, then top the orzotto with the sausages. Sprinkle with chilli flakes, grate over plenty of Parmesan and drizzle with more olive oil before serving.

olive oil, for frying, plus extra to serve

6 vegan sausages, sliced diagonally into chunks

2 tbsp wholegrain mustard

1½ tbsp agave syrup

3 tbsp vegan butter

2 leeks, finely sliced

300g (10½oz) orzo

4 garlic cloves, minced

1 tsp dried thyme

150ml (⅔ cup) white wine (ensure vegan)

1 litre (4⅓ cups) hot vegetable stock

200g tenderstem broccoli, roughly chopped

400g (14oz) can white beans, drained and rinsed

100ml (6½ tbsp) vegan single (light) cream

2 tbsp nutritional yeast

zest and juice of ½ lemon

dried chilli (red pepper) flakes, to serve

vegan Parmesan, to serve

salt and freshly ground black pepper

Prep	Cook	Difficulty level	Protein per serving
5 mins	35–40 mins	2/5	22.3g (¹³⁄₁₆oz)

Charred Cauli Traybake *with* Cauli Leaf Pesto

Serves 2

Nothing screams comfort more than a one-pan self-care dinner with minimal washing up. Using the cauliflower leaves in the pesto makes this a zero-waste recipe too!

Preheat the oven to 200°C (180°C fan/400°F/Gas 6).

Place the cauliflower florets and leaves in a large roasting pan. Toss with a drizzle of oil and a generous pinch of salt then roast for 15 minutes. Remove the cauliflower leaves from the tray and place to one side.

Reduce the oven temperature to 190°C (170°C fan/375°F/Gas 5). Add the butter beans, tomatoes, onion and broccoli to the roasting pan with the florets, then dust over the caraway, cumin and paprika and season well with salt and pepper. Drizzle with a little more oil, toss well and roast for another 20–25 minutes until the veggies are tender and a little charred in places.

Meanwhile, roughly chop the roasted cauliflower leaves (discarding any stringy bits or very tough stems) and place them in a blender or food processor along with the remaining pesto ingredients. Blitz until smooth, adding a splash of water if needed to help it blend.

Top the traybake with spoonfuls of the pesto, then crumble over the feta and scatter with basil leaves before serving immediately.

1 small head cauliflower (about 500g/18oz), outer leaves removed and head broken into small, even-sized florets

olive oil, for drizzling

400g (14oz) can butter (lima) beans, drained and rinsed

200g (7oz) cherry tomatoes

1 red onion, cut into wedges

150g (5½oz) tenderstem broccoli

1 tsp ground caraway seeds

1 tsp ground cumin

1 tbsp smoked paprika

vegan feta, to serve

salt and freshly ground black pepper

FOR THE CAULI LEAF PESTO

roasted cauliflower leaves (from the cauliflower, above)

handful of basil leaves, plus extra to serve

1 garlic clove

juice of ½ lime

3 tbsp jarred jalapeños

3 tbsp olive oil

2 tbsp nutritional yeast

pinch of salt

Courgette *(kind of)* Carbonara

Serves 4

Courgettes are so versatile, and they don't get enough credit – you'd never guess that they make up the base of this ultra-silky sauce. They're the perfect "hidden vegetable" and in this recipe ensure a much healthier alternative to a cream-based sauce.

Set a large frying pan (skillet) over a medium heat and drizzle in some oil. Add the courgette, onion and garlic and sauté for 10 minutes until everything is lightly browned and softened.

Transfer the contents of the pan to a blender or food processor then add the remaining sauce ingredients. Blitz until smooth then leave to one side.

Boil the pasta according to the packet instructions until al dente, then drain, reserving a cupful of pasta water.

Meanwhile, set the frying pan back over a medium heat and fry the lardons until golden and crispy. Remove about a third of the lardons from the pan and set them aside, then add the sauce and the pasta to the pan.

Reduce the heat to low and toss gently to combine everything, adding pasta water to loosen the sauce if needed.

Serve in bowls topped with the reserved lardons, a drizzle of olive oil and some more freshly ground black pepper.

400g (14oz) spaghetti or linguine (ensure vegan)

200g (7oz) vegan bacon lardons

drizzle of olive oil, plus extra to serve

FOR THE SAUCE

2 small courgettes (zucchinis), peeled and roughly chopped

1 white onion, roughly chopped

5 cloves garlic, roughly chopped

400ml (1⅔ cups) oat milk

60g (2¼oz) meltable smoked vegan cheese

juice of ½ lemon

4 tbsp nutritional yeast

2 tbsp apple cider vinegar

1 tbsp white miso paste

1 tsp freshly ground black pepper, plus extra to serve

Prep	Cook	Difficulty level	Protein per serving
5 mins	25 mins	2/5	13.7g (½oz)

Hug-in-a-bowl Date Stew

Serves 4

Rich, aromatic, spicy and sweet, this one-pan wonder is ready in under 30 minutes but tastes like you've been simmering it for hours.

Place a casserole dish over a low heat and drizzle in some olive oil. Add the onion and pepper and sweat for 5 minutes until starting to soften. Add the dates, garlic and ginger and stir through. Season well with salt and pepper then stir in the garam masala, paprika and harissa paste and fry for 1 minute until aromatic.

Deglaze the dish with vinegar then tip in the plum tomatoes, breaking them apart with your hands as you add them. Fill the can with water then add that to the dish too. Add the borlotti beans then give everything a good mix. Bring back to a simmer then leave to simmer for 10 minutes.

Taste the stew and season with salt and pepper as needed, then add the frozen spinach and cook for a further 5–10 minutes, stirring occasionally, until the spinach has thawed.

Serve the stew with dollops of yogurt on top and some flaked almonds and lemon zest sprinkled over, and with flatbreads on the side for dunking and scooping.

drizzle of olive oil

1 red onion, finely sliced

1 red (bell) pepper, deseeded and diced

4 large Medjool dates, roughly chopped

3 garlic cloves, minced

2.5cm (1in) piece of fresh root ginger, minced

1 tsp garam masala

1 tsp smoked paprika

1½ tbsp rose harissa paste

1 tbsp red wine vinegar

400g (14oz) can plum tomatoes

400g (14oz) can borlotti beans, drained and rinsed

125g (4½oz) frozen spinach

salt and freshly ground black pepper

TO SERVE

4 tbsp soya yogurt

handful of toasted flaked almonds

zest of 1 lemon

2 Turkish or Persian flatbreads, halved

Harissa Celeriac + Tofu Skewers *with* Jewelled Couscous

Serves 4 *(makes 8 skewers)*

An underused root vegetable, celeriac is actually a great flavour sponge along with (my fave) tofu. These skewers are sticky, spicy and a perfect match for the fruity and sweet couscous.

Preheat your oven to 220°C (200°C fan/425°F/Gas 7) and line a baking sheet with baking parchment. Alternatively, preheat your air fryer to 200°C (400°F) and spray or drizzle the basket with vegetable oil.

Combine the glaze ingredients in a large bowl then add the celeriac and tofu pieces and gently toss to coat, ensuring each piece is completely covered in the glaze.

Grab 8 wooden skewers (trim them to fit your air fryer if needed) and thread each with 6–8 pieces of celeriac and tofu, alternating as you do so. Place the skewers on the lined baking sheet or in the greased air fryer basket and cook for 15–20 minutes, flipping them halfway, until charred at the edges.

Meanwhile, to make the jewelled couscous, place a saucepan over a medium heat and add the olive oil. When hot, add the onion and fry for 5 minutes until beginning to soften, then add the garlic, cinnamon and cumin and fry for a further 1 minute. Add the couscous and vegetable stock and simmer for about 10 minutes, stirring regularly, until all the stock has been absorbed. Stir through the parsley, lemon juice, raisins and dried apricots then season with salt and pepper to taste.

Pile the couscous onto a large serving plate then top with the skewers. Dollop over some yogurt and sprinkle with pomegranate seeds and a little extra parsley before diving in.

½ celeriac (celery root), peeled and cut into 2.5cm (1in) cubes

225g (8oz) extra-firm tofu, drained and cut into 2.5cm (1in) cubes

FOR THE GLAZE

2 tbsp harissa

3 tbsp vegetable oil, plus extra for drizzling/spraying

1 tsp balsamic vinegar

1 tsp dried oregano

1 tsp smoked paprika

½ tsp ground cumin

½ tsp ground coriander seeds

¼ tsp ground cinnamon

FOR THE JEWELLED COUSCOUS

2 tbsp olive oil

1 red onion, finely chopped

4 garlic cloves, minced

1 tsp ground cinnamon

1 tbsp ground cumin

250g (9oz) giant couscous

800ml (generous 3¼ cups) hot vegetable stock

handful of parsley, chopped, plus extra to serve

juice of ½ lemon

small handful of raisins

small handful of dried apricots, chopped

TO SERVE

vegan yogurt

pomegranate seeds

Prep	Cook	Difficulty level	Protein per serving
10 mins	30 mins	3/5	24.5g (⅞oz)

Tofu + Walnut Bolognese

Serves 4

People go back to this recipe time and time again and I don't blame them! This has all the "meatiness" you could want from a Bolognese without any ultra-processed ingredients.

Preheat your oven to 210°C (190°C fan/410°F/Gas 6–7) and line a baking sheet with baking parchment. Alternatively, preheat your air fryer to 190°C (375°F) and spray or drizzle the basket with oil.

Add 2 tablespoons of olive oil to a large frying pan (skillet) set over a medium heat. When hot, add the carrot, celery, onion and garlic and fry for 5 minutes until everything has a little colour.

Stir in the tomato purée and fry for another minute, then add the bay leaves, dried mixed herbs and paprika and season well with salt and pepper. Stir to combine then deglaze the pan with the balsamic vinegar, scraping up any brown bits from the bottom of the pan.

Next add the plum tomatoes, crushing them with your hands or a spoon as you add them. Fill one empty can with water and add that in along with the stock cube, sugar and soy sauce. Reduce the heat to low and leave to simmer for about 10 minutes.

Meanwhile, to make the shredded tofu "meat", coarsely grate the tofu using a box grater then combine on the lined baking sheet or in the air fryer basket with the soy sauce and olive oil, ensuring the tofu is nicely coated. Bake for 20 minutes or air fry for 15 minutes, tossing regularly as it catches quickly. Add the walnuts for the final 5 minutes. When cooked, the tofu should be medium brown and slightly crispy and the walnuts lightly charred. Add the tofu to your simmering sauce, along with the oat milk, then stir everything well and taste for seasoning.

Cook your pasta to al dente, according to packet instructions, then toss it with the ragù before serving in bowls. Sprinkle with parsley and some chopped walnuts to finish, if you like. Alternatively, you can grate the walnuts using a microplane to mimic Parmesan.

2 tbsp olive oil, plus extra for greasing

1 carrot, finely chopped

2 celery sticks, finely chopped

1 red onion, finely chopped

4 garlic cloves, minced

2 tbsp tomato purée (paste)

2 bay leaves

1 tbsp dried mixed herbs

1 tbsp smoked paprika

2 tbsp balsamic vinegar

2 x 400g (14oz) cans plum tomatoes

1 vegetable stock cube

1 tsp soft light brown sugar

1 tbsp dark soy sauce

3½ tbsp oat milk

salt and freshly ground black pepper

FOR THE SHREDDED TOFU "MEAT"

220g (8oz) extra-firm tofu, drained

1 tbsp dark soy sauce

2 tbsp olive oil

50g (1¾oz) walnuts, finely chopped, plus extra to serve (optional)

TO SERVE

350g (12oz) pasta of your choice (ensure vegan)

parsley, roughly chopped

Prep	Cook	Difficulty level	Protein per serving
15 mins	30–35 mins (+ cooling)	4/5	7.3g (¼oz)

Elly's Welly

Serves 8

Perfect for a Christmas spread, this Wellington is also lovely as a summer-style Sunday roast (as pictured). Packed with extra fibre and goodness from the lentils, you'll be left with clean plates after everyone has dug in.

Combine the stuffing mix with the water in a large bowl and leave to hydrate for 5 minutes. Next add all the remaining filling ingredients to the bowl, season well with salt and pepper and mix well. Using your hands is useful here to squish the sausages and ensure everything is completely combined.

Preheat your oven to 210°C (190°C fan/410°F/Gas 6–7) and line a baking sheet with baking parchment.

Lay the puff pastry sheet onto the lined baking sheet then pile the filling mixture along one long side of the pastry, leaving a slight gap at either end. Compact the filling into an even log shape, then fold the pastry over it and crimp the edges with your fingers or a fork to completely enclose the filling.

Mix the olive oil and maple syrup together in a small bowl, then brush this all over the Wellington. Sprinkle it with the nigella seeds then bake the Wellington for 30–35 minutes until golden brown. Leave to stand for 15 minutes then slice and serve with garlic Parm roasties, sweet chilli carrots, lamb's lettuce and plenty of tomato relish.

320g (11oz) store-bought ready-rolled puff pastry (ensure vegan)

2 tsp olive oil

1 tsp maple syrup

1 tsp nigella seeds

salt and freshly ground black pepper

FOR THE FILLING

60g (2oz) vegan stuffing mix

100ml (6½ tbsp) water

8 vegan sausages (the "meaty" kind), casings removed

400g (14oz) can lentils, drained and rinsed

75g (2½oz) dried cranberries, chopped

zest of ½ lemon

small handful of thyme, leaves picked and chopped

small handful of rosemary, leaves picked and chopped

1 tsp smoked paprika

TO SERVE

garlic Parm roasties (page 61)

sweet chilli carrots (page 56)

lamb's lettuce

store-bought tomato relish

NOTE

If you can't get hold of vegan stuffing mix, use the same weight of fresh breadcrumbs seasoned with 1 tbsp dried mixed herbs. If doing this, you may not need all the water specified – add enough water to hydrate the breadcrumbs until they are sticky but not wet.

Prep	Cook	Difficulty level	Protein per serving
10 mins	45 mins	3/5	17.5g (⅝oz)
(+ overnight marination)			

Sticky Tofu Fillet *with* Red Wine Jus

Serves 4

It's easy to get impatient when something needs marinating but, trust me, this one is worth waiting for! All the prep time is in the marinating here so it's deceptively easy to make. The rich umami flavours in the finished product make this one of my favourite recipes.

Place the stock in a saucepan set over a medium heat. Once boiling, add the block of tofu to the pan and boil for 3 minutes (if the stock doesn't fully cover the tofu, flip it over after 1½ minutes).

Drain the tofu over a bowl, reserving 200ml (scant 1 cup) of stock. When cool enough to handle, and using a sharp knife, halve the block lengthways then slice a criss-cross pattern halfway into each piece – this will help the marinade to penetrate it.

Place all the marinade ingredients into a sealable container, along with the reserved stock, and whisk until combined. Add the tofu to the marinade, seal the lid and leave in the fridge to marinate overnight (or for up to 2 days).

When ready to cook, preheat your oven to 220°C (200°C fan/ 425°F/Gas 7).

Grease a small baking dish with a glug of olive oil, then remove the tofu from the marinade and transfer it to the dish. Pour the marinade into a small saucepan and set over a low heat. Cook and reduce for 15–20 minutes, stirring occasionally, until you have a thick and glossy jus. Bake the tofu for 45 minutes, basting with the jus every 15 minutes.

Serve the tofu in slices with some new potatoes, shallots and tenderstem broccoli (or your fave veggies) and any remaining jus.

400ml (1¾ cups) vegan beef stock

400g (14oz) block extra-firm tofu, drained

glug of olive oil

FOR THE MARINADE

3 tbsp light soy sauce

175ml (¾ cup) red wine

1½ tbsp vegan Worcestershire sauce

1½ tbsp dark brown sugar

1½ tbsp tomato purée (paste)

1 tbsp nutritional yeast

1 tsp ground cumin

1½ tsp smoked paprika

1 tsp Marmite (or other yeast extract)

TO SERVE

roasted new potatoes

roasted shallots

steamed tenderstem broccoli

Prep	Cook	Difficulty level	Protein per serving
15 mins	1 hour	4/5	28.4g (1oz)

Lasagne *with* White Bean Béchamel

Serves 6

Making a classic lasagne can really pile up the dirty dishes. That's why this one uses a speedy no-cook white sauce. The beans here add creaminess and a big boost of fibre too. You can't go wrong! (Find my other no-fuss, one-pan lasagne recipe on page 142).

First, make the filling. Heat 1 tablespoon of the oil in a deep, lidded frying pan (skillet) set over a medium heat. Once hot, add the vegan minced beef and fry for 5–7 minutes until browned, then transfer to a bowl and set aside.

Place the pan back on the heat, then add the remaining 1 tablespoon of olive oil, followed by the onion, carrot, celery, mushrooms and garlic. Season well with salt and pepper and fry for 8–10 minutes until catching and slightly browned.

Pour in the vinegar to deglaze the pan, then add the remaining ingredients, crushing the plum tomatoes by hand as you add them. Give everything a good stir and allow to come back up to temperature, then reduce the heat to low, cover and simmer for 20 minutes until the lentils are soft. Add the vegan minced beef back to the pan and stir to combine. Taste, adding salt and pepper if needed, then remove from the heat and discard the bay leaves.

Preheat your oven to 220°C (200°C fan/425°F/Gas 7).

To make the white sauce, simply add all the ingredients to a blender (including the liquid from one of the cans of white beans) and blitz until smooth. Taste and add more salt and pepper if needed.

250g (9oz) lasagne sheets (ensure vegan)

200g (7oz) meltable vegan Cheddar, grated

salt and freshly ground black pepper

FOR THE FILLING

2 tbsp olive oil

250g (9oz) vegan beef mince (vegan ground beef)

1 onion, finely chopped

1 carrot, finely chopped

2 celery sticks, finely chopped

6 chestnut (cremini) mushrooms, finely chopped

4 garlic cloves, minced

2 tbsp red wine vinegar or balsamic vinegar

400g (14oz) can of plum tomatoes

small handful of basil, chopped

2 bay leaves

1 tbsp dried mixed herbs

1 tbsp smoked paprika

2 tbsp tomato purée (paste)

1 tbsp dark soy sauce

1 tbsp Marmite (or other yeast extract)

100g (½ cup) dried red lentils

300ml (1¼ cups) vegan beef stock (or use vegetable stock)

→

Continued...

Grab a baking dish about 30 x 20cm (11 ¾ x 8in) in size. Spoon a third of the filling into the dish in an even layer then top with some lasagne sheets, avoiding any overlap (snap them if needed). Spoon in another layer of filling, drizzle over a third of the white bean béchamel, sprinkle with a third of the grated Cheddar, then add another layer of lasagne sheets. Repeat this once more (filling, bechamel, cheese, pasta), then finish by topping the final set of lasagne sheets with the remaining third of béchamel and grated cheese.

Place the baking dish on a baking sheet to catch any overflow while it cooks, then transfer the lasagne to the oven to bake for 35–45 minutes, or until the top is golden and bubbling. Remove from the oven and allow to sit for 10 minutes before serving with a green salad.

FOR THE WHITE BEAN BÉCHAMEL

2 x 400g (14oz) cans white beans; 1 can drained and rinsed, 1 can still with its liquid

250ml (1 cup) oat milk

juice of ½ lemon

1 tbsp white miso paste

1 tsp English mustard

4 tbsp nutritional yeast

½ tsp onion powder

½ tsp garlic powder

½ tsp ground black pepper

½ tsp salt

Double Mushroom Brisket + Lentil Ragù

Serves 4

Even if you're a mushroom hater, please just stay with me for this one. Drying the mushrooms out in the pan totally changes their texture and gives such a "meaty" vibe to this ragù – try it and I promise you'll love it.

Place the dried shiitake mushrooms in a heatproof bowl and pour over the boiling water to just cover the mushrooms. Set aside to rehydrate for 30 minutes then drain (reserving the soaking liquid) and roughly chop.

Place a casserole dish over a medium–high heat and add the oyster mushrooms with a pinch of salt. Fry for about 10 minutes, pressing the mushrooms with a spatula to help release water. Once the water has cooked off and they are dry (and sound a bit squeaky when you mix them), add the cumin, paprika, soy sauce and agave syrup and mix well.

Stir in 1 tablespoon of the oil then scrape any extra flavour and charred bits from the bottom of the dish using a spatula. Cook for a further 2 minutes then transfer the oyster mushrooms to a plate and set aside.

Place the dish back over a medium heat and add the remaining 1 tablespoon of oil. Add the onions, carrot and celery and sweat for 10 minutes until they start to caramelize. Add the garlic and rehydrated shiitake mushrooms then cook for 2 more minutes before deglazing the pan with the red wine.

Tip in the lentils, along with the liquid from the can, and the plum tomatoes, breaking them apart with your hands as you add them. Crumble in the stock cube, then add the Marmite, bay leaves and the liquid used to rehydrate the shiitake mushrooms. Stir everything well then place the lid on the dish and reduce the heat to low–medium.

5 dried shiitake mushrooms

100ml (⅓ cup) boiling water

300g (10½oz) oyster mushrooms, torn into thin strips

1 tsp ground cumin

1 tsp smoked hot paprika

1 tbsp dark soy sauce

1 tsp agave syrup

2 tbsp olive oil

1 onion, finely chopped

1 carrot, finely chopped

1 celery stick, finely chopped

3 garlic cloves, minced

120ml (½ cup) red wine (ensure vegan)

400g (14oz) can brown or green lentils, including the liquid from the can

400g (14oz) can plum tomatoes

1 reduced-salt vegetable stock cube

1 heaped tsp Marmite (or other yeast extract)

2 bay leaves

300g (10½oz) green beans, to serve

salt and freshly ground black pepper

Comforting Plates

169

Continued...

Simmer for 30 minutes, stirring every 10 minutes, then add the oyster mushrooms back to the casserole dish.

Meanwhile, make the butter bean mash. Set a large saucepan over a medium heat and add the butter. Once the butter has melted, add the butter beans, Cheddar and lemon juice and cook for about 5 minutes, crushing the beans with a wooden spoon as they soften. Using a hand-held blender, blitz the beans until smooth. Season with salt and pepper to taste then stir through the chives. Keep warm.

Set a steamer over a pan of boiling water and steam the green beans for about 5 minutes until tender.

Serve the ragù over the butterbean mash with the green beans on the side.

FOR THE BUTTERBEAN MASH

2 tbsp vegan butter

4 x 400g (14oz) can butter (lima) beans, drained and rinsed

100g (3½oz) meltable vegan Cheddar, grated

juice of 1 lemon

small handful of chives, finely chopped

Butter Chickpea Curry

Serves 4

This is traditionally a rich and indulgent dish, but my vegan version is one you can eat daily, and it's a firm favourite in our house. Perfect for meal prepping during an extra-busy week!

Place the cashew nuts in a small heatproof bowl and cover with boiling water from the kettle. Leave to soften for 20 minutes.

Meanwhile, melt the butter in a saucepan set over a medium heat. Add the onion and gently cook for 10 minutes until softened. Stir in the garlic and ginger and cook for another 2 minutes, then tip in the tomatoes and cinnamon stick and cook for a further 8 minutes. Add the tomato purée and all the remaining spices, mix well, then remove from the heat.

Remove the cinnamon stick from the pan. Drain the cashew nuts then add them to the pan along with the cream (reserving a little of the cream for serving). Use a hand-held blender to blitz the mixture until smooth (or transfer everything to a food processor or blender).

Add the chickpeas to the sauce and set back over a low heat to ensure everything is warm through. Serve over rice with a drizzle of the reserved cream and some coriander scattered over.

50g (1¾oz) cashew nuts

2 tbsp vegan butter

1 onion, finely chopped

3 garlic cloves, minced

2.5cm (1in) piece fresh root ginger, minced

3 plum tomatoes, roughly chopped

½ cinnamon stick

1½ tbsp tomato purée (paste)

1 tsp garam masala

1 tsp (Kashmiri) chilli powder (adjust to your spice tolerance)

½ tsp dried fenugreek leaves

½ tsp ground turmeric

½ tsp ground cumin

250ml (1 cup) vegan single (light) cream

2 x 400g (14oz) cans chickpeas, drained and rinsed

cooked basmati rice, to serve

small handful coriander (cilantro), roughly torn

Creamy Coconut + Tofu Noodle Soup

Serves 2

My most viral recipe for good reason – this is perfect if you're short on time (and energy) but still want a delicious, soupy, hug-in-a-bowl that tastes like it's been simmering for hours. I don't know why it took me so long to discover that you can grate tofu... more surface area equals more flavour!

Preheat your oven or air fryer to 200°C (180°C fan/400°F/Gas 6).

Grate (shred) the tofu using the coarse side of a box grater then transfer it to a baking sheet. Add the dark soy sauce, agave syrup and 1 tablespoon of the sesame oil and toss to coat. Bake for 18 minutes or air fry for 12 minutes, tossing regularly, until crispy. Place to one side.

Meanwhile, add the vegetable oil to a lidded frying pan (skillet) set over a medium heat. When hot, add the pak choi to the pan cut-side down and apply pressure with a spatula. Cook for 3 minutes until lightly golden, then flip, pop on the lid and cook for a further 3 minutes. Remove from the heat and set aside. Alternatively, simply tear and add the tender pak choi leaves (discarding the stem) straight to the broth during the final 3 minutes of cooking time.

Heat the remaining 1 tablespoon of sesame oil in a large saucepan set over a medium heat then add the spring onions, coriander stalks, garlic and ginger and fry for 5 minutes. Next add the miso paste, light soy sauce and shiitake mushrooms. Crumble in the stock cube then add the coconut milk and water (add more or less water depending on how brothy you want your noodles). Bring to the boil then immediately reduce the heat to low and simmer for 10 minutes. Stir in the lime juice then remove from the heat.

Cook the noodles according to the packet instructions, then drain. Divide the noodles between bowls, then pour over the broth. Add some pak choi and crispy tofu to each bowl. Garnish with coriander leaves, chilli oil and serve with lime wedges on the side for squeezing.

200g (7oz) extra-firm tofu, drained

1 tbsp dark soy sauce

1½ tsp agave syrup

2 tbsp sesame oil

1 tbsp vegetable oil

250g (9oz) pak choi (bok choy), tough end removed and halved lengthways

4 spring onions (scallions), chopped

small handful of coriander (cilantro), leaves picked and stalks finely chopped

2 garlic cloves, minced

2.5cm (1in) piece of fresh root ginger, minced

1 tbsp white miso paste

1 tbsp light soy sauce

6 dried shiitake mushrooms, rehydrated and sliced

1 vegan chicken stock cube

200ml (scant 1 cup) coconut milk

400–600ml (1¾–2½ cups) water

juice of 1 lime, plus extra wedges to serve

200g (7oz) dried noodles of your choice (ensure vegan)

chilli oil, to serve

Messy
Plates

The one you've all
been waiting for...
napkins at the ready
for the best burgers
of your life.

Hot Honey Halloumi Burger
180
Crispy Satay Burger
184
Barbie Beet Burger
186
Buffalo Shroom Burger
189
Beer-Battered Fish Burger
190
Reuben Sandwich
192
Ultimate Smash Burger
194
Smoky Pulled Aubergine Burger
197

Prep	Cook	Difficulty level	Protein per burger
20 mins (+ marinating)	35 mins	3/5	31.7g (1oz)

Hot Honey Halloumi Burger

Serves 2

A true fan favourite and my most recreated burger. Who can resist that moreish sweet and spicy balance of flavours? If you haven't tried prebaking your tofu before breading it then you have to give this a go; it really helps to recreate a halloumi-style texture.

To make the tofu halloumi, add all the ingredients (apart from the tofu) to a sealable container and stir well. Now add the tofu, ensuring it is completely covered in the marinade, then seal the lid and leave in the fridge to marinate for 30 minutes (or up to 2 days).

To make the slaw, simply combine all ingredients in a large bowl and refrigerate until ready to serve.

To make the hot honey, add the maple syrup to a saucepan set over a low heat. When it starts to bubble add the chilli flakes and remove the pan from the heat. Allow to infuse for 5 minutes, stirring regularly, then pour into a jug or jar and set aside.

Preheat your oven to 220°C (200°C fan/425°F/Gas 7) and line a baking sheet with baking parchment. Alternatively, preheat your air fryer to 190°C (375°F) and spray or drizzle the basket with vegetable oil.

Remove the tofu patties from the marinade and place on the lined baking sheet or in the greased air fryer basket. Cook for 20 minutes, flipping them over halfway.

FOR THE TOFU HALLOUMI

juice of 1 lemon

2 tbsp olive oil

2 tbsp nutritional yeast

1 tsp dried oregano

1 tsp dried mint

1 tsp garlic powder

1 tsp salt

1 tsp freshly ground black pepper

225g (8oz) block extra-firm tofu, drained and cut into 2 equal square-shaped patties

FOR THE SLAW

¼ cucumber, finely sliced into ribbons (a swivel peeler is useful)

1 carrot, grated

¼ white cabbage, finely sliced

½ red onion, finely sliced

juice of ½ lemon

2 tbsp vegan mayo

1 tbsp apple cider vinegar

1 tbsp maple syrup

1 tsp salt

FOR THE HOT HONEY

80ml (5½ tbsp) maple syrup

1 tsp dried chilli (red pepper) flakes

1 tsp hot paprika

$\longrightarrow$

Continued...

Grab 3 shallow bowls for the coating: place the plain flour in one bowl; combine the water, cornflour, oregano, mint and garlic powder in another bowl; then place the panko breadcrumbs, sesame seeds and a pinch each of salt and pepper in the final bowl. Stir each bowl well.

When the tofu is cool enough to handle, place each patty in the flour bowl, ensuring they are evenly dusted. Next, dip the patties into the bowl with the wet mixture to fully coat. Finally add them to the breadcrumbs bowl and lightly toss to coat – you may need to press the breadcrumbs onto the tofu to coat the patties fully.

Place the coated patties back in the air fryer at 190°C (375°F), spray or drizzle them with a little oil and air fry for 15 minutes until crisp and golden, flipping them halfway. Alternatively, shallow fry them in a little oil in a frying pan (skillet) set over a medium heat for about 5 minutes, flipping as needed until crisp.

Now you can assemble! Add a little mayo to the bases of the brioche buns, then top each with a halloumi patty. Drizzle over some hot honey, add some slaw then finish with the bun tops.

FOR THE COATING

3 tbsp mixed sesame seeds

50g (generous 1 cup) panko breadcrumbs

2 tbsp cornflour (cornstarch)

1 tsp dried oregano

1 tsp dried mint

1 tsp garlic granules

80ml (5 tbsp) water

2 tbsp plain (all-purpose) flour

TO SERVE

2 vegan brioche burger buns (or your favourite roll), split and toasted

2 tbsp vegan spicy mayo

Messy Plates

Prep	Cook	Difficulty level	Protein per burger
20 mins (+ marinating and chilling)	6 mins	3/5	44.8g (1½oz)

Crispy Satay Burger

Serves 4

Move over breadcrumbs because this coating makes these burgers a textural triumph. Cornflakes aren't just for breakfast.

Combine all the satay sauce ingredients in a bowl and mix until smooth. Taste and season with salt and pepper.

Place the tofu triangles in a sealable container and toss with half the satay sauce (you may need to add a little water to thin out the satay sauce to help it coat the tofu). Seal the lid and leave in the fridge to marinate for 30 minutes (or overnight).

Grab three shallow bowls: place the plain flour in one bowl; add the milk to another bowl; then add the peanuts and cornflakes to the final bowl, scrunching them with your hands to break down the cornflakes a little. Season each bowl with some salt and pepper.

Place each patty in the flour bowl, ensuring they are evenly dusted. Next, dip the patties into the bowl with the milk to fully coat. Finally add them to the cornflake and peanut bowl and lightly toss to coat – you may need to press the pieces onto the tofu to coat the patties fully. Place the coated patties onto a small tray or plate and transfer them to the fridge for 30 minutes.

Heat the vegetable oil in a deep-sided frying pan (skillet) set over a medium heat. Once hot (test by adding a pinch of cornflakes – if they sizzle and turn golden in 30 seconds the oil is ready), fry the patties for about 3 minutes on each side until golden all over.

Spoon the remaining satay sauce onto the bases of each toasted brioche bun. Layer on some cucumber ribbons, coriander leaves and pickled red onions then top with a crispy patty. Squeeze on some spicy mayo then finish with the bun tops.

2 x 250g (9oz) blocks extra-firm tofu, each drained and halved into 2 patties

100g (¾ cup) plain (all-purpose) flour

200ml (¾ cup) dairy-free milk

160g (1¼ cups) peanuts, finely chopped

100g (4 cups) cornflakes (ensure vegan)

250ml (1 cup) vegetable oil, for shallow frying

salt and freshly ground black pepper

FOR THE SATAY SAUCE

4 tbsp smooth peanut butter

juice of 1 lime

1 tbsp dark soy sauce

1 tbsp rice wine vinegar

1 tbsp sesame oil

1 tsp agave syrup

1 tsp curry powder

TO SERVE

4 vegan brioche burger buns (or your favourite roll), split and toasted

1 cucumber, sliced into ribbons

small handful of coriander (cilantro) leaves

store-bought pickled red onions

4 tbsp vegan spicy mayo

NOTE

You can also cook the patties in your air fryer. Spray all over with oil, then air fry at 190°C (375°F) for about 12 minutes, flipping them halfway.

Prep	Cook	Difficulty level	Protein per burger
20 mins (+ chilling)	40 mins	3/5	14.2g (½oz)

Barbie Beet Burger

Serves 4

The recipe that converted me to veggie burgers for good. Imagine a classic veggie burger, reimagined with great bite and made pink (honestly, what's not to love?).

Preheat the oven to 220°C (200°C fan/425°F/Gas 7).

Slice the top off the garlic bulb and place it on a sheet of foil. Drizzle it with some olive oil and season with a pinch of salt then wrap the foil around it and bake for 25–30 minutes until soft.

Meanwhile, cook the spelt according to the packet instructions, then drain and set aside.

Grate the beetroot onto a baking sheet then add the onion and butter beans. Season with salt and pepper, toss well and roast for 10 minutes. Remove from the oven and leave to cool.

Now make the sumac radishes. Simply combine all the ingredients in a bowl and mix well. Refrigerate until ready to serve.

Once the garlic bulb is cool enough to handle, squeeze the flesh into a food processor and add the cooked spelt, beetroot, onions and butterbeans, the breadcrumbs, cornflour, capers, mayo, lemon zest and mint, along with plenty of salt and pepper. Blitz until semi-smooth.

Now make the feta crème fraîche. Simply combine all the ingredients in a bowl, season with salt and pepper and mix well.

Split the burger mixture into 4 equal patties then place them in the fridge for 30 minutes. Set a large frying pan (skillet) over a medium heat and drizzle with some oil. When hot, add the patties and season the tops with salt and pepper. Cook for 4–5 minutes then flip and cook for another 3 minutes, or until golden brown on both sides.

Add some sumac radishes to the toasted buns, then top with a patty, the feta crème fraîche and some salad cress.

1 garlic bulb

olive oil, for drizzling

60g (2¼oz) spelt

100g (3½oz) cooked beetroot (not the type in vinegar)

½ red onion, finely chopped

400g (14oz) can butter (lima) beans, drained and rinsed

60g (generous ½ cup) fine golden breadcrumbs

1 tbsp cornflour (cornstarch)

1 tbsp capers

1 tbsp vegan mayo

zest of ½ lemon

3 mint sprigs, leaves picked and finely chopped

4 seeded burger buns (ensure vegan), split and toasted

salad cress, to serve

salt and freshly ground black pepper

FOR THE SUMAC RADISHES

100g (3½oz) pink radishes, thinly sliced

2 tbsp olive oil

2 tbsp apple cider vinegar

1 tbsp agave syrup

1 tsp sumac

1 tsp salt

FOR THE FETA CRÈME FRAÎCHE

150g (¾ cup) vegan crème fraîche

100g (3½oz) vegan feta

juice of ½ lemon

pinch of dried chilli (red pepper) flakes

Buffalo Shroom Burger

Serves 2

Buffalo sauce is a god-tier hot sauce, and yes, I will die on this hill. No surprise then that this burger is a favourite of mine. The oyster mushrooms have an unreal bite when paired with the puffed rice. Honestly, if this photo doesn't make you want to dive in then I don't know what will!

Start by making the ranch slaw. Add all ingredients to a bowl and mix well. Season with salt and pepper and refrigerate until ready to serve.

Preheat your oven to 210°C (190°C fan/410°F/Gas 6–7) or your air fryer to 190°C (375°F).

Grab two bowls: add the puffed rice cereal, paprika, dried mixed herbs, onion powder, garlic powder, cumin and ½ teaspoon of black pepper to the first bowl; add the milk, lemon zest and 2 tablespoons of the plain flour to the second bowl. Season both bowls with salt and mix well. Crush some of the puffed rice cereal with your hand, so about half of it is crushed and the rest is whole.

Dust the remaining 1 tablespoon of plain flour over the mushrooms.

Using one hand for wet and one for dry, dip the mushrooms into the wet mixture to fully coat them. Now dip them into the dry mixture, pressing it onto the mushrooms to ensure they are fully coated.

Place the coated mushrooms on a baking sheet or into your air fryer basket and drizzle with a little oil. Bake in the oven for 12–14 minutes or air fry for 8–10 minutes, flipping halfway, until crispy.

Meanwhile make the buffalo glaze. Melt the butter in a small saucepan then stir in the buffalo sauce and warm through. Add the crispy mushrooms and briefly stir to coat.

Add some gherkins to the base of your toasted buns then layer on the glazed mushrooms. Top with slaw then add the bun tops and devour.

60g (2¼ cups) puffed rice cereal (ensure vegan)

1 tsp paprika

1 tsp dried mixed herbs

½ tsp onion powder

½ tsp garlic powder

½ tsp ground cumin

75ml (⅓ cup) dairy-free milk

zest of ½ lemon

3 tbsp plain (all-purpose) flour

200g (7oz) large oyster mushrooms

vegetable oil, for drizzling

sliced gherkins (pickles), to serve

2 vegan brioche burger buns (or your favourite roll), split and toasted

salt and freshly ground black pepper

FOR THE RANCH SLAW

¼ small white cabbage, shredded

1 spring onion (scallion), shredded or finely sliced

handful of flat-leaf parsley, roughly chopped

handful of dill, roughly chopped

1 garlic clove, minced

juice of ½ lemon

2 tbsp vegan mayo

1 tbsp vegan crème fraîche

FOR THE BUFFALO GLAZE

2 tbsp vegan butter

1 tbsp buffalo hot sauce

Prep	Cook	Difficulty level	Protein per burger
30 mins (+ freezing)	5 mins	4/5	20.9g (¾oz)

Beer-Battered Fish Burger

Serves 2

Tofu is beautifully versatile, but it does need help when it comes to recreating that perfect flaky fish. Enter: artichokes. Jarred artichokes maintain a neutral flavour while imitating the flaky texture we need for a full fish burger experience.

To make the "fish" patties, finely crumble the tofu into a bowl and add all the remaining ingredients (apart from the cornflour). Mix everything thoroughly, then add the cornflour and mix again. Form two equal round patties then place them on a small baking sheet lined with baking parchment. Place in the freezer until frozen solid (overnight is best).

Combine all the ingredients for the tartare sauce in a small bowl. Mix well and place in the fridge until ready to serve.

When ready to cook, heat the vegetable oil in a large saucepan to 180°C (350°F), ensuring it comes no more than two-thirds up the sides of the pan.

To make the batter, add the plain flour to a bowl along with the baking powder, beer and some salt and pepper and whisk until smooth. To another shallow dish add the 2 tablespoons of plain flour for dusting.

Remove the patties from the freezer. Working one at a time, add a patty to the flour bowl to dust it all over, then dip it into the batter, ensuring it is completely coated. Immediately (but carefully) lower it into the hot oil and fry until golden (around 4 minutes). Remove from the oil with a slotted spoon and transfer to a wire rack or plate lined with kitchen paper. Repeat with the second patty then sprinkle both with a little salt.

Spoon some tartare sauce onto the base of your buns and add a handful of rocket. Top each with a "fish" patty, more tartare sauce and gherkin slices. Add the bun tops and enjoy.

about 1 litre (1 quart) vegetable oil, for deep frying

2 vegan brioche burger buns (or your favourite roll), split and toasted

small handful of lettuce

2 gherkins (pickles), sliced

salt and freshly ground black pepper

FOR THE "FISH" PATTIES

150g (5½oz) smoked extra-firm tofu, drained

50g (1¾oz) cooked artichoke hearts in oil, drained and chopped

handful of dill, finely chopped

zest and juice of ½ lemon

1 sheet of nori, finely crushed

1 tbsp nutritional yeast

½ tbsp pickle juice (from the gherkin jar)

1 tsp white miso paste

½ tsp garlic powder

½ tsp onion powder

2 tbsp cornflour (cornstarch)

FOR THE BATTER

45g (5½ tbsp) plain (all-purpose) flour, plus 2 tbsp for dusting

1 tsp baking powder

175ml (¾ cup) chilled beer (ensure vegan) or sparkling water

FOR THE TARTARE SAUCE

4 tbsp vegan mayo

juice of ½ lemon

small handful of dill, chopped

1 gherkin (pickle), finely chopped

1 tsp capers, finely chopped

1 tsp pickle juice (from the gherkin jar)

Reuben Sandwich

Serves 2

This sandwich is a real contender for my favourite recipe in this book – just look at those layers! Peeling your tofu is the trick to nailing this recipe, and you can leave it marinating in the fridge for days for maximum flavour payoff and easy sandwich assembly.

Using a swivel peeler, shave the block of tofu into thin slices. If this starts to get a little tricky towards the end of the block, simply cut the remaining tofu into slices as thinly as possible. In a sealable container, whisk together the remaining tofu pastrami ingredients, then add the tofu to the marinade, seal the lid and leave in the fridge to marinate for 1 hour (or up to 2 days).

When you're ready to cook, preheat the oven to 210°C (190°C fan/410°F/Gas 6-7) and line a baking sheet with baking parchment.

Spread out the marinated tofu on the lined baking sheet then cook for 20–30 minutes, flipping the tofu over halfway to ensure it becomes evenly brown.

Meanwhile, combine all the dressing ingredients in a bowl and season with salt and pepper if needed.

Spoon some dressing onto two slices of the toasted sourdough, add some rocket, then pile on the tofu pastrami. Add gherkins and some sauerkraut to each, then finish with a little more dressing and top with the remaining slices of toasted sourdough.

FOR THE TOFU PASTRAMI

220g (8oz) smoked extra-firm tofu, drained

100ml (6½ tbsp) beetroot juice

1 tbsp olive oil

1½ tsp balsamic vinegar

1 tbsp white miso paste

1 tsp Marmite (or other yeast extract)

½ tsp English mustard

1 tsp liquid smoke (optional)

½ tbsp soft light brown sugar

1 tbsp smoked paprika

1 tsp onion powder

FOR THE DRESSING

3 tbsp vegan mayo

1 tbsp ketchup

½ tbsp hot sauce

1½ tsp English mustard

½ tsp smoked paprika

½ tsp garlic powder

TO SERVE

4 slices of sourdough bread, toasted

handful of rocket (arugula)

4 gherkins (pickles), sliced

handful of sauerkraut

Ultimate Smash Burger

Serves 2

Forgo the store-bought patty with hundreds of ingredients you can't pronounce and instead make one from scratch that looks just as good as (if not better than) the real deal! The ultimate vegan burger – no frills, no fuss.

First, make the smash patties. Place the TVP in a heatproof bowl and pour over the hot stock. Set aside for 10 minutes to allow it to absorb all the liquid.

Combine the breadcrumbs and milk in a large mixing bowl and leave to soak for a couple of minutes.

Remove the TVP from the bowl, squeezing out as much liquid as possible, then add it to the breadcrumb bowl along with the remaining ingredients (apart from the vital wheat gluten) and mix well. Now add the vital wheat gluten and a pinch of salt and knead for 8–10 minutes.

Divide the mixture into 4 even-sized balls, rolling them between your palms. Place the balls on a baking sheet lined with baking parchment then flatten each one into a patty about 10cm (4in) wide. Cover and refrigerate for about 15 minutes, or until ready to cook.

For the burger sauce, simply combine all the ingredients in a small bowl and taste for seasoning, adding salt and pepper as needed.

Add a drizzle of vegetable oil to a frying pan (skillet) set over a medium heat. When hot, add a patty to the pan (you may be able to cook 2 at a time depending on the size of your frying pan) and fry for 3 minutes. Using a spatula, flip the patty and add a slice of burger cheese to the cooked side. Add a splash of water to the pan then immediately cover with a lid for 30 seconds to melt the cheese.

Add some burger sauce to the bases of your toasted buns. Stack 2 patties in each burger and top with more sauce, some lettuce and plenty of gherkins.

4 slices of vegan burger cheese

2 sesame-topped burger buns (ensure vegan), split and toasted

handful of shredded lettuce

small handful of sliced gherkins (pickles)

salt and freshly ground black pepper

FOR THE SMASH PATTIES

50g (2oz) TVP mince (page 14)

100ml (⅓ cup) hot vegetable stock

30g (¾ cup) panko breadcrumbs

2 tbsp dairy-free milk

1 large garlic clove, minced

20g (¾oz) solid coconut oil

1 tbsp nutritional yeast

1 tbsp Marmite (or other yeast extract)

2 tsp gravy granules (ensure vegan)

1½ tsp smoked paprika

1 tsp browning (for colour; optional)

½ tsp onion powder

½ tsp freshly ground black pepper

30g (¼ cup) vital wheat gluten

FOR THE BURGER SAUCE

1 tbsp chopped gherkins (pickles)

1 small garlic clove, minced

3 tbsp vegan mayo

1½ tbsp tomato ketchup

1 tsp English mustard

Prep	Cook	Difficulty level	Protein per burger
20 mins	1 hour 10 mins	4/5	12.6g (⁷⁄₁₆oz)

Smoky Pulled Aubergine Burger

Serves 4

When I tried cooking aubergine like this for the first time I was blown away! And used in this burger it is heavenly – trust me, you'll never look at aubergine the same way again.

Preheat the oven to 220°C (200°C fan/425°F/Gas 7) and line a baking sheet with baking parchment.

Place the aubergines on the baking sheet and prick all over with a fork. Drizzle with a little oil and season with salt and pepper. Roast for 20 minutes until soft then transfer to a large bowl and cover with a clean tea towel (dish towel). Leave to one side for 10 minutes.

Reduce the oven temperature to 200°C (180°C fan/400°F/Gas 6).

In a small bowl mix together the BBQ sauce ingredients until fully combined.

Once cool enough to handle, halve the aubergines and peel away the skin. Slice the flesh into long thin strips and place back onto a lined baking sheet. Brush half the BBQ sauce onto the aubergine strips, until they are completely coated on all sides, then drizzle with a little oil. Roast for 40–50 minutes, tossing every 10 minutes, until dark and caramelized.

Meanwhile prepare the apple slaw by combining all the ingredients in a large bowl along with plenty of salt and pepper. Next, make the herby mayo by combining the mayo and herbs in a small bowl.

To assemble your burger, add a cheese slice to the toasted bun then top with a quarter of the pulled aubergine, some extra BBQ sauce and a couple of slices of cooked bacon. Add some apple slaw then finish with a spoonful of the herby mayo and a little fresh dill before adding the burger top.

4 aubergines (eggplants)

vegetable oil, for drizzling

4 vegan brioche burger buns (or your favourite roll), split and toasted

4 slices vegan burger cheese

8 slices cooked vegan bacon (I use La Vie)

salt and freshly ground black pepper

FOR THE BBQ SAUCE

2 tbsp BBQ seasoning

2 tbsp soft dark brown sugar

4 tbsp tomato ketchup

2 tsp white vinegar

2 tsp sweet smoked paprika

½ tsp ground cayenne pepper

FOR THE APPLE SLAW

1 green apple, julienned

1 carrot, peeled and julienned

¼ white cabbage, shredded

2 spring onions (scallions), shredded or finely sliced

juice of ½ lemon

FOR THE HERBY MAYO

4 tbsp vegan mayo

small handful of chives, finely chopped

small handful of dill, finely chopped, plus extra to serve

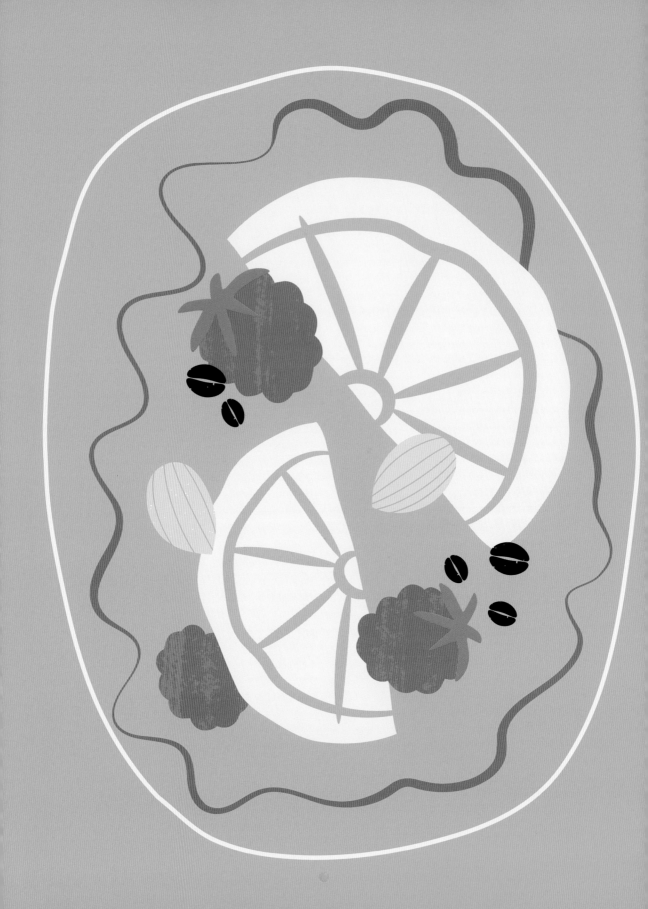

8

Sweet
Plates

Six recipes to satisfy every sweet craving and occasion. Even as a savoury girl I can't resist these...

Raspberry + Almond Crumble Bars
202
Lemon Drizzle Chia Cookies
204
Date + Dark Chocolate Banana Bread
206
Salted Almond Brownies
208
Miso + Pecan Skillet Cookie
211
Espresso Martini Chocolate Churros
214

Raspberry + Almond Crumble Bars

Makes 12

A feel-good dessert, these sweet treats are a perfect everyday snack as they have so much added goodness: fibre from the oats, loads of healthy minerals from the almonds and Vitamin C from the raspberries.

Preheat the oven to 190°C (170°C fan/375°F/Gas 5) and line a 20cm (8in) square baking tin (pan) with baking parchment.

In a large bowl place the flour, sugar, oats, baking powder, cubed butter and a pinch of salt. Use your fingertips to rub the mixture together until it resembles coarse crumbs and there is no butter left.

In a separate bowl, use a fork to stir together all the raspberry filling ingredients (apart from the almond butter), until some of the raspberries begin to break down.

Transfer two-thirds of the crumble mixture to the baking tin and press it into the tin firmly and evenly (using the base of a glass helps here). Pour the raspberry mixture on top and spread it out evenly. Drizzle the almond butter on top of the raspberry filling, then sprinkle over the remaining crumble mixture.

Sprinkle over flaked almonds then bake for 35–40 minutes until golden. Leave to cool completely before slicing into 12 squares.

FOR THE CRUMBLE

160g (1¼ cups) plain (all-purpose) flour

100g (½ cup) soft light brown sugar

120g (1¼ cups) rolled oats (oatmeal)

½ tsp baking powder

150g (1¼ sticks) cold vegan butter, cubed

pinch of salt

50g (⅔ cup) flaked (slivered) almonds

FOR THE RASPBERRY FILLING

300g (10½oz) raspberries

1 tbsp cornflour (cornstarch)

zest and juice of 1 lemon

2 tbsp caster (superfine) sugar

3 tbsp almond butter

Lemon Drizzle Chia Cookies

Makes 8

One of the simplest bakes you can make, I had to include these cookies in the book for my mum (aka the world's biggest lemon drizzle cake fan). Quicker to make than the traditional loaf and absolutely perfect for a grab and go sweet treat.

Preheat your oven to 200°C (180°C fan/400°F/Gas 6) and line a baking sheet with baking parchment.

Add the chia seeds and 3 tablespoons of water to a small bowl and mix. Set aside for a few minutes until it has a jelly-like consistency.

In a mixing bowl, combine the lemon zest and both sugars. Add the butter, chia mixture, vanilla extract and half the lemon juice and cream together using a wooden spoon.

Briefly combine the flour and baking powder in a separate bowl, then scrape the wet mixture into the flour bowl and mix until just combined.

Roll the cookie dough into 8 equal balls (each about 70g/2½oz) then place them on the lined baking sheet. Top each ball with a thin slice of lemon, if you like. Bake for 12–15 minutes, until they have spread and are very lightly golden, then transfer to a wire rack to cool.

Mix the icing sugar and remaining lemon juice together until smooth, then drizzle this over the cooled cookies. Allow to set before eating.

1 tbsp chia seeds

zest and juice of 2 lemons, plus extra very thin half-slices of lemon to decorate (optional)

100g (½ cup) caster (superfine) sugar

50g (¼ cup) soft light brown sugar

100g (6½ tbsp) vegan butter, softened

1 tsp vanilla extract

225g (1¾ cups) plain (all-purpose) flour

1 tsp baking powder

50g (⅓ cup) icing (confectioners') sugar

Date + Dark Chocolate Banana Bread

Serves 8

A good banana loaf must be super-moist. That's where dates come in, keeping the cake soft and meaning we can add less refined sugar too. Win-win. Toast a slice of this and slather it with vegan butter for a beautiful afternoon pick-me-up.

Preheat your oven to 210°C (190°C fan/410°F/Gas 6–7). Grease a 450g (1lb) loaf tin (about 20.5 x 10cm/8 x 4in).

Place the dates and water in a small saucepan set over a medium–high heat. When the water comes to the boil, reduce the heat and simmer for 10 minutes until the dates have fully softened. Remove from the heat, add the bicarbonate of soda then use a hand-held blender to blitz the mixture to a purée.

In a large mixing bowl, mash the bananas using a fork, then stir in the yogurt, lemon juice and sunflower or vegetable oil. In another large bowl, combine the flour, sugar, baking powder, cinnamon, nutmeg, salt and chocolate.

Add the dry mix to the bowl with the mashed bananas and stir to fully combine, then fold in the date purée until everything is just mixed.

Tip the batter into the greased loaf tin and bake for 45–50 minutes, or until a skewer inserted into the centre of the loaf comes out clean. Keep an eye on the banana bread as it bakes – if the top gets too dark simply cover it with foil while it continues baking.

Remove from the oven and allow to cool in the tin for 10–15 minutes before turning out onto a wire rack. Serve warm or at room temperature, sliced and spread with vegan butter, or topped with yogurt and your favourite berries. This will keep for up to 5 days in an airtight container.

200g (7oz) pitted Medjool dates

300ml (1¼ cups) water

1 tsp bicarbonate of soda

2 ripe bananas (about 240g/8½oz)

170g (6oz) soy yogurt

juice of ½ lemon

3½ tbsp sunflower or vegetable oil, plus extra for greasing

270g (2 cups) self raising (rising) flour

100g (½ cup) soft light brown sugar

1 tsp baking powder

1 tsp ground cinnamon

½ tsp ground nutmeg

½ tsp fine sea salt

150g (5½oz) dark chocolate (ensure vegan), roughly chopped

vegan butter, to serve (optional)

vegan yogurt and berries, to serve (optional)

Salted Almond Brownies

Makes 9–12

Brownies can be hard to get right (there's nothing worse than a "cakey" brownie) but you can't miss with this gooey recipe. You can keep them plain if you like, by simply omitting the nuts, but this salted almond version is out of this world.

Preheat the oven to 210°C (190°C fan/410°F/Gas 6–7) and line a 20cm (8in) square baking tin (pan) with baking parchment.

Melt the chocolate and baking block in a heatproof bowl set over a saucepan or in the microwave in 20 second bursts. Once melted, stir in the yogurt, sugar, vanilla extract and flaxseed mixture until completely combined.

Sift the flour, cocoa powder and a pinch of salt into a large mixing bowl. Pour the chocolate mixture into the flour and stir until just combined.

Scrape the mixture into your lined baking tin, ensuring the top is level, then scatter with the almonds and chocolate chips and sprinkle with a little flaky sea salt. Bake for 25 minutes.

Remove from the oven, allow to cool completely then transfer to the fridge (still in the tin) for a couple of hours until completely set.

Remove from the tin and slice into 9 or 12 brownies. These will be very fudgy! They will keep in the fridge in a sealed container for up to 5 days – I like to let them sit at room temperature for 15 minutes before eating.

225g (8oz) dark chocolate (ensure vegan)

120g (1 stick) vegan baking block

260g (scant 1¼ cups) soya yogurt

250g (1¼ cups) soft light brown sugar

1 tbsp vanilla extract

4 tbsp ground flaxseed mixed with 4 tbsp water

200g (1½ cups) self raising (rising) flour

20g (¼ cup) unsweetened cocoa powder

100g (3½oz) almonds, roughly chopped

100g (3½oz) vegan chocolate chips

flaky sea salt

Miso + Pecan Skillet Cookie

Serves 4

No need to stress about that dinner party dessert when you have this one-pan showstopper to hand. Nutty pecans and salty miso are such a match made in heaven! I honestly wish I could eat it for breakfast (maybe I will...).

Preheat the oven to 200°C (180°C fan/400°F/Gas 6) and grease a 20cm (8in) skillet with a little vegan butter.

In a mixing bowl, cream together the butter, sugars, miso paste and vanilla using a wooden spoon or electric hand whisk. Once light and fluffy, beat in the flaxseed mixture.

In a separate bowl combine the flour, baking powder, pecan nuts and chocolate chips.

Tip the dry mixture into the wet mixture and stir until just combined – don't overmix!

Scrape the mixture into the skillet and press down in an even layer. Bake for 20–25 minutes, or until golden brown on top. Serve warm topped with the vanilla ice cream and lots of spoons for digging in.

110g (1 stick) vegan butter, plus extra for greasing

75g (¼ cup) soft light brown sugar

100g (½ cup) caster (superfine) sugar

1 tbsp white miso paste

1 tsp vanilla extract

1 tbsp ground flaxseed mixed with 3 tbsp water

180g (1¾ cups) plain (all-purpose) flour

1 tsp baking powder

80g (¾ cup) chopped pecan nuts

80g (½ cup) vegan chocolate chips

4 scoops vegan vanilla ice cream, to serve

Sweet Plates

Espresso Martini Chocolate Churros

Serves 6

An ode to my love of profiteroles and espresso martinis, this mash-up dessert is ready for when you need to pull out the big guns. Paired with the perfect after-dinner cocktail your guests won't be able to stop thinking about it (and neither will you).

First make the dough for the churros. In a large bowl combine the plain flour, baking powder, sugar and salt.

In a saucepan set over a medium heat, warm the soya milk and butter until the butter has melted and the liquid is just simmering.

Pour the hot liquid over the dry mixture and beat using a wooden spoon or electric hand whisk until fully combined. Cover with a clean tea towel or cloth and set aside to cool slightly.

Meanwhile, mix together the sugar and espresso powder in a shallow bowl to create your coffee sugar. Set aside.

For the chocolate sauce, place the chocolate in a heatproof bowl. Combine the cream and sugar in a saucepan set over a medium heat, stirring to dissolve the sugar. Once it's simmering, pour the cream over the chocolate. Wait for 30 seconds, then pour in the espresso and whisk the mixture until smooth and glossy. Cover and set aside.

To make the Kahlua cream, whisk together the cream and Kahlua using an electric hand whisk until soft peaks form. Set aside.

Place the vegetable oil in a large, deep-sided saucepan, ensuring it comes no more than two-thirds up the sides of the pan, and heat to between 160–180°C (325–350°F).

about 1 litre (1 quart) vegetable oil (for deep frying)

coffee beans, to serve

FOR THE CHURROS

250g (generous 1¾ cups) plain (all-purpose) flour

2 tsp baking powder

20g (1½ tbsp) golden caster (superfine) sugar

¼ tsp salt

50g (3½ tbsp) vegan butter

300ml (1¼ cups) soya milk

FOR THE COFFEE SUGAR

100g (½ cup) golden caster (superfine) sugar

2 tsp espresso powder

FOR THE CHOCOLATE SAUCE

200g (7 oz) dark chocolate (ensure vegan), chopped

150ml (⅔ cup) vegan double (heavy) cream

4 tbsp golden caster (superfine) sugar

2 x double shot of strong espresso

FOR THE KAHLUA CREAM

125ml (½ cup) vegan double (heavy) cream

2 tbsp Kahlua

$\longrightarrow$

Continued...

Fit a piping bag with a large star nozzle and fill the bag with the churro batter.

Once the oil is hot enough, hold the piping bag a few inches above the oil and carefully pipe 4–6 churros directly into the oil, snipping the batter with scissors in between each one. Aim for the churros to be 6–8cm (2¼–3¼in) long – you should get about 30 churros. Fry them for 1–2 minutes until golden, then remove the churros from the oil using a slotted spoon and transfer to a plate lined with kitchen paper to drain off any excess oil. When still hot, add the churros to the bowl of coffee sugar and toss to coat. Repeat until all the churros are cooked and coated.

Now to assemble everything! Add a few spoonfuls of chocolate sauce to a dessert glass, top with 5 churros, then finish with a dollop of Kahlua cream and some coffee beans. Repeat to fill the other 5 glasses then serve.

Index

A

agave syrup 13
almond butter: chocolate protein pots 39
   raspberry + almond crumble bars 202
almonds: salted almond brownies 208
artichoke hearts: hummus pasta 74
   beer-battered fish burger 190
aubergines (eggplants): smoky pulled aubergine burger 197
   sticky pomegranate aubergine 44

B

bacon, vegan: courgette (kind of) carbonara 154
   one pan full English 26
   smoky pulled aubergine burger 197
bananas: date + dark chocolate banana bread 206
Barbie beet burger 186
beans 13
   kimchi beans 70
   lasagne with white bean béchamel 167–68
   smoky sausage mockmuffins 34
   three-bean chorizo chilli 100
   see also individual types of bean
béchamel, white bean 167–68
beer-battered fish burger 190
beetroot: Barbie beet burger 186
black beans: best ever burrito 138
   gochujang + black bean loaded sweet potatoes 89
Bolognese, tofu + walnut 160
boozy butter beans + greens 30
bread: Reuben sandwich 192
   whipped ricotta toast 22
   see also burgers; flatbreads; wraps
breakfast frittata 32
broccoli: miso + lemon broccoli with whipped spring onion tofu 52
brownies, salted almond 208
buffalo shroom burger 189
burgers: Barbie beet burger 186
   beer-battered fish burger 190
   buffalo shroom burger 189
   crispy satay burger 184

   hot honey halloumi burger 180–83
   smoky chorizo burger 102
   smoky pulled aubergine burger 197
   ultimate smash burger 194
burrito, best ever 138
butter, vegan 16
butter (lima) beans: Barbie beet burger 186
   boozy butter beans + greens 30
   kimchi beans 70
butternut squash croquettes with harissa crème 62

C

Caesar chickpea pitta pockets 72
cakes: date + dark chocolate banana bread 206
   salted almond brownies 208
cannellini beans: cannellini, cheese + chive tarts 84
   seitan chicken 113
carbonara, courgette (kind of) 154
carrots, sweet chilli 56
cashew nuts: cashew slaw 128
   garlic Parm roasties 61
cauliflower: charred cauli traybake with cauli leaf pesto 153
celeriac: harissa celeriac + tofu skewers with jewelled couscous 158
cheese, vegan 16
   cannellini, cheese + chive tarts 84
   cheesy kale 54
   cheesy ramen with crispy mushrooms 148
   rice paper omelette 37
chicken, vegan 14
   green skillet lasagne 142
   lime + lemongrass noodle bowl 118
   seitan chicken 113
   spinach, ricotta + chicken quesadillas 114
   Thai green chicken curry 120
   Tuscan chicken pie 116
chickpeas: butter chickpea curry 172
   Caesar chickpea pitta pockets 72
   crispy gnocchi with Romesco hummus 82
   Thai-style fish cakes 65
chilli jam tahini noodles 140

chillies: sweet chilli carrots 56
   three-bean chorizo chilli 100
chimichurri: mushroom + jackfruit chimichurri
   tacos 80
chocolate: chocolate protein pots 39
   date + dark chocolate banana bread 206
   espresso martini chocolate churros 214–16
   salted almond brownies 208
chorizo, tofu: smoky chorizo burger 102
   smoky tofu chorizo tacos 96
   three-bean chorizo chilli 100
   tofu chorizo 95
churros, espresso martini chocolate 214–16
coconut: coconut tofu with spicy mango sauce 78
coconut milk: creamy coconut + tofu noodle soup
174
cookies: lemon drizzle chia cookies 204
   miso + pecan skillet cookie 211
courgette (kind of) carbonara 154
couscous, jewelled 158
cream, vegan 16
   peaches + cream pancakes 24
crispy spiced filo rolls 48
croquettes: squash croquettes with harissa crème
62
crumble bars, raspberry + almond 202
cucumbers, nutty smashed 51
curry: butter chickpea curry 172
   Thai green chicken curry 120

D
dairy alternatives 16
dates: date + dark chocolate banana bread 206
   hug-in-a-bowl date stew 156

E
edamame beans: coconut tofu with spicy mango
sauce 78
Elly's Welly 162
English muffins: smoky sausage mockmuffins 34
equipment 17
espresso martini chocolate churros 214–16

F
filo (phyllo) pastry: crispy spiced filo rolls 48
"fish": beer-battered fish burger 190
   Thai-style fish cakes 65
flatbreads: herby gyros with tzatziki 131
   'nduja flatbreads 77
fries: herby gyros with tzatziki 131

frittata, breakfast 32
full English, one pan 26

G
garlic parm roasties 61
gnocchi: crispy gnocchi with Romesco hummus 82
gochujang + black bean loaded sweet potatoes 89
gyros: herby gyros with tzatziki 131

H
halloumi burger, hot honey 180–83
harissa: harissa celeriac + tofu skewers with
   jewelled couscous 158
   squash croquettes with harissa crème 62
herbs 13
hummus: crispy gnocchi with Romesco hummus 82
   hummus pasta 74

I
ingredients 13–16

J
jackfruit: mushroom + jackfruit chimichurri
tacos 80
   Thai-style fish cakes 65

K
kale, cheesy 54
kimchi beans 70

L
lahmacun-inspired smashed tacos 134
lasagne: green skillet lasagne 142
   lasagne with white bean béchamel 167–68
leek + sausage orzotto 150
lemons: lemon drizzle chia cookies 204
   lemon pepper mushroom wings 46
   miso + lemon broccoli with whipped spring
      onion tofu 52
lentils: double mushroom brisket + lentil ragù
169–70
   Elly's welly 162
lime + lemongrass noodle bowl 118
loaded and spicy omelette 37

M
Manchurian meatball noodles 106
mango sauce, spicy 78
maple syrup 13
Marmite 13

mayonnaise, lemon mustard 46
meat alternatives 14
meatballs: Manchurian meatball noodles 106
  mega protein meatballs 104
peppercorn meatballs + mash 110
  spaghetti meatballs with rocket + mint pesto 108
milk, vegan 16
mince, vegan 14
  crispy spiced filo rolls 48
  lasagne with white bean béchamel 167–68
miso paste 13
  miso + lemon broccoli with whipped spring
    onion tofu 52
  miso + pecan skillet cookie 211
mockmuffins, smoky sausage 34
mushrooms 14
  buffalo shroom burger 189
  cheesy ramen with crispy mushrooms 148
  double mushroom brisket + lentil ragù 169–70
  lemon pepper mushroom wings 46
  mushroom + jackfruit chimichurri tacos 80
  one pan full English 26

N
'nduja flatbreads 77
noodles: chilli jam tahini noodles 140
  creamy coconut + tofu noodle soup 174
  lime + lemongrass noodle bowl 118
  Manchurian meatball noodles 106
  peanut + sesame soba salad 136
nori 13
nutritional yeast 13

O
olives: hummus pasta 74
omelettes, rice paper 37
onions, quick pickled 131

P
pancakes, peaches + cream 24
pasta: courgette (kind of) carbonara 154
  green skillet lasagne 142
  hummus pasta 74
  lasagne with white bean béchamel 167–68
  leek + sausage orzotto 150
  spaghetti meatballs with rocket + mint pesto 108
  tofu + walnut Bolognese 160
pastrami, tofu: Reuben sandwich 192
peaches + cream pancakes 24
peanut butter: crispy satay burger 184

nutty smashed cucumbers 51
  peanut + sesame soba salad 136
peas: green skillet lasagne 142
pecans: miso + pecan skillet cookie 211
pesto: cauli leaf pesto 153
  rice paper omelette 37
  rocket + mint pesto 108
pie, Tuscan chicken 116
pitta pockets, Caesar chickpea 72
pomegranate juice: sticky pomegranate aubergine 44
potatoes: garlic parm roasties 61
  mash 110
protein pots, chocolate 39
puff pastry: Elly's welly 162
pulses 13

Q
quesadillas, spinach, ricotta + chicken 114
quinoa: reset quinoa bowl with tofu feta 126

R
ragù, double mushroom brisket + lentil 169–70
ramen: cheesy ramen with crispy mushrooms 148
raspberry + almond crumble bars 202
Reuben sandwich 192
rice: coconut tofu with spicy mango sauce 78
rice paper omelette 37
Romesco hummus, crispy gnocchi with 82

S
salad, peanut + sesame soba 136
salt 12, 13
  salted almond brownies 208
sandwiches, Reuben 192
satay burgers, crispy 184
sausages, vegan 14
  Elly's welly 162
  leek + sausage orzotto 150
  'nduja flatbreads 77
  one pan full English 26
  smoky sausage mockmuffins 34
seitan chicken 113
  lime + lemongrass noodle bowl 118
  spinach, ricotta + chicken quesadillas 114
  Thai green chicken curry 120
  Tuscan chicken pie 116
skewers, harissa celeriac + tofu 158
slaw, cashew 128
smoky sausage mockmuffins 34
soup, creamy coconut + tofu noodle 174

spices 13
spinach: boozy butter beans + greens 30
  breakfast frittata 32
  green skillet lasagne 142
  smoky sausage mockmuffins 34
  spinach, ricotta + chicken quesadillas 114
spring onions: miso + lemon broccoli with
  whipped spring onion tofu 52
squash croquettes with harissa crème 62
stew, hug-in-a-bowl date 156
sticky pomegranate aubergine 44
stock cubes 13
sweet chilli carrots 56
sweet potatoes, gochujang + black bean loaded 89

T
tacos: lahmacun-inspired smashed tacos 134
  mushroom + jackfruit chimichurri tacos 80
  smoky tofu chorizo tacos 96
tahini: chilli jam tahini noodles 140
tarts, cannellini, cheese + chive 84
tempeh 14
textured vegetable protein (TVP) 14
  best ever burrito 138
  lahmacun-inspired smashed tacos 134
  mega protein meatballs 104
  ultimate smash burger 194
Thai green chicken curry 120
Thai-style fish cakes 65
tofu 14
  beer-battered fish burger 190
  breakfast frittata 32
  chocolate protein pots 39
  coconut tofu with spicy mango sauce 78
  creamy coconut + tofu noodle soup 174
  crispy satay burger 184
  harissa celeriac + tofu skewers with jewelled
couscous 158
  hot honey halloumi burger 180–83
  mega protein meatballs 104
  miso + lemon broccoli with whipped spring
   onion tofu 52
  rice paper omelette 37
  seitan chicken 113
  spinach, ricotta + chicken quesadillas 114
  sticky hasselback tofu with cashew slaw 128
  sticky tofu fillet with red wine jus 164
  tofu + walnut Bolognese 160
  tofu chorizo 95
  tofu feta 126

tofu pastrami 192
  tofu scramble 26
  whipped ricotta toast 22
tofu chorizo 95
  smoky chorizo burger 102
  smoky tofu chorizo tacos 96
  three-bean chorizo chilli 100
tofu feta, reset quinoa bowl with 126
tofu pastrami: Reuben sandwich 192
tomatoes: one pan full English 26
  smoky tomato sauce 34
tortillas: best ever burrito 138
  lahmacun-inspired smashed tacos 134
  spinach, ricotta + chicken quesadillas 114
traybake: charred cauli traybake with cauli leaf
  pesto 153
Tuscan chicken pie 116
tzatziki 131

U
ultimate smash burger 194

V
vital wheat gluten 14

W
walnuts: tofu + walnut Bolognese 160
Wellington: Elly's welly 162
whipped ricotta toast 22
wine: sticky tofu fillet with red wine jus 164

Y
yogurt, dairy-free 16
  cumin yogurt 48
  sticky pomegranate aubergine 44
  tzatziki 131

Thank You

To my partner Jem; unfortunately the word count won't stretch to the paragraphs you truly deserve. Your constant support and unwavering belief in my abilities was the reason this journey began. I would never have quit my job and followed my passions without you. No dream was ever too big in your eyes (and no plate ever too big to polish off). You are my "why" for many things in life and I can't quite thank you enough for this one.

To my sister Grace for being my biggest cheerleader since day one (not sure who you championed more, me or my tofu chorizo). Despite being one of the fussier eaters I know, you still try everything I make and tell me it is the best thing on earth.

To my mum, thank you for thinking everything I do is the best thing since sliced bread. Your calm encouragement during my daily (correction: hourly) phone calls is the reason this book is finished in one piece. I would be a very lost lamb without you. To my dad, for encouraging every hobby I've ever had in life, which has likely led me to this path. Thank you for shouting about all my endeavours with such pride to anyone and everyone that will listen. You are both the best parents in the world.

To the best in-laws anyone could want; Clare and Arthur you are two of the kindest people on earth. Thank you for constantly bigging me up to people far and wide. And to my sister-in-law Ella, thank you for putting every single one of my recipes "in your top five". You are the best recipe tester.

To all of my gorgeous friends over the years, but especially to Nic for listening to every wild creative concept I've had, travelling to shoots just to cheer me on, championing me and building me up every single day… God I love you. Thank you to my incredible housemates Aimee and Hayley who ate my endless creations (hard job but someone's gotta do it) with even more enthusiastic feedback than the last. To Tom, for the last-minute headshots, constant editing advice and for being both the best hype man and the calm voice of reason. I love you all SO much.

To Gaz, from when we met all the way back in 2018, you have been instrumental in my journey. I can't thank you enough for how much you've inspired me, and especially for your lovely words on the cover of this book. I'm so lucky to call you a friend.

To everyone I've met on this wild social media journey but especially to Issy, Nat, Clare, Ebony and Giuseppe. From the moment I told you all about this I was met with nothing but pure support and constant words of wisdom. You are all the most incredibly supportive people I could've ever wished to have met during this wild ride and I'm so blessed to be surrounded by such incredible energy that's pushed me to consistently reach for higher things.

To the whole DDA crew but especially to my manager Taome, my right arm, I would never have pushed myself out of my comfort zone without your constant affirmations and amazing ideas. So much of this is your doing just as much as mine.

To my literary agent Oscar, thank you for making all of this possible! For your reassurance and patience in my slightly erratic ways and for managing to quash my constant imposter syndrome.

To everyone at DK – Cara, Lucy and Tania – thank you for bringing my vision to life and executing things I didn't know were possible! Nothing has been too big of an ask or too unachievable. You have made this experience a total dream.

To my editor Harriet, I might not have finished this in one piece without you! You have the patience of a saint and have been such a rock throughout this whole journey from start to finish; I can't thank you enough.

To Jo and Saskia (and Pepper!), I don't think I could've dreamed up a better shoot team. You both made me feel so capable and confident on set and just like a part of the family. I never thought I could have such a ball while shooting ten recipes a day (the sensational playlists definitely helped). I will forever be grateful (and in awe) of how beautiful these photos are.

To Alice and Caitlin, your food testing and development wizardry made this book possible in the tight and often stressful time constraints we had! You both just fully got the vision and had so much kindness and patience towards me. You're both 10/10 babes!

To the best prop team, Daisy and Théa, thank you for making me want to steal every piece of cutlery and crockery on set, and dealing with my every whim and last minute set changes.

To Nikki from NicandLou, my incredible designer, I don't know how you brought every part of my vision to life so perfectly but I could not be more in love with this book if I tried, you are incredible!

To everyone that has followed Elly's Plate since its conception, this would not exist without you and I am SO grateful. The community we have constantly makes me feel so inspired and complete. Thank you for making all of my dreams become reality.

About the Author

Elly Smart quit a career in law to pursue a life in food. She worked in vegan donut shops, as well as alongside Gaz Oakley on his YouTube channel, before starting a role as Development Chef at The Vurger Co where she created their entire menu, producing best-selling specials, and later developing a product range that sold in Ocado. Elly became a full-time content creator in 2023 and focuses on creating plant-based comfort food without restriction, ensuring everyone's plate is always packed with flavour.

PUBLISHER'S ACKNOWLEDGMENTS

DK would like to thank Caitlin Nuala and Alice Katie Hughes for their help with food styling and recipe development, and Théa Carter for prop styling assistance. Thanks to Kerry Torrens for providing information on protein content, to John Friend for proofreading and to Vanessa Bird for indexing.

A NOTE ON NUTRITIONAL INFORMATION

Nutritional information is provided as a guide only. This information may vary due to several factors. These include the accuracy of weights and measures, variations in cooking and preparation, product brands used, as well as the seasonality of fresh produce.

DK LONDON

Editorial Director Cara Armstrong
Senior Editor Lucy Sienkowska
Senior Designer Tania Gomes
Senior Production Editor Tony Phipps
Senior Production Controller Stephanie McConnell
DTP and Design Coordinator Heather Blagden
Jackets and Sales Material Coordinator Emily Cannings
Art Director Maxine Pedliham

Editorial Harriet Webster
Design Nikki Dupin and Beth Free for Studio Nic & Lou
Photography Jo Sidey
Prop styling Daisy Shayler-Webb
Food styling Saskia Sidey

First American Edition, 2024
Published in the United States by DK RED, an imprint of DK Publishing, a division of Penguin Random House LLC
1745 Broadway, 20th Floor, New York, NY 10019

Published in Great Britain by Dorling Kindersley Limited

A catalog record for this book is available from the Library of Congress.

ISBN 978-0-5939-6737-9

Printed and bound in Latvia

www.dk.com

MIX
Paper | Supporting responsible forestry
FSC™ C018179

This book was made with Forest Stewardship Council™ certified paper – one small step in DK's commitment to a sustainable future. Learn more at www.dk.com/uk/information/sustainability